The Engine of Destiny

Cosmopsychology

Marc Robertson

Copyright 1976 Marc Robertson
All rights reserved.

No part of this book may be reproduced or transmitted in any form or by any means, electronic or mechanical, including photocopying or recording, or by any information storage and retrieval system, without written permission from the author and publisher. Requests and inquiries may be mailed to: American Federation of Astrologers, Inc., PO Box 22040, Tempe, AZ 85284-2040.

ISBN: 978-086690-693-7

Cover Design: Celeste Nash-Weninger
First Printing: 1976
Current Printing: 2024

Published by:
American Federation of Astrologers, Inc.
PO Box 22040
6535 S. Rural Road
Tempe, AZ 85285-2040

Printed in the United States of America

Contents

Preface   v

1 - Most of Us Are Asleep   1

2 - Our God Is Science Now   7

3 - But We Are Waking   15

4 - To A New Vision   21

5 - Reading the Cycle in Lives   27

6 - The Planets in Pairs   37

7 - Ahead and Behind   83

Preface

Not long ago, I decided to call what I'm teaching and practicing cosmopsychology rather than the traditional name of astrology. I did this because of the unfortunate popular connotations associated with the old word and partly because the new name described more accurately what I was attempting to formulate in my own mind and get across to others—a view of ourselves in a cosmic setting (rather than a social, moral, national, racial, or political setting) that was founded upon a psychological approach to the individual rather than a success- or failure-oriented view of him.

Every practitioner of astrology or any other arcane system of viewing people has, whether he will admit it or not, a prestructured idea of what he is trying to see through a person and his makeup in light of the elements that surround him.

I don't think a lot of the people who work with these things actually think about it, but half of what they do and probably eighty percent of what they say, is highly prejudiced, as well as prestructured, by this view (which they may realize or not realize consciously), which amounts to a position taken on what they are attempting to see or find out.

At the very outset, therefore, I am willing to state what I am searching for in applying astrology to an individual or his life. when I look at a birth chart, and consider the person who has brought me a particular problem which he hopes the birth chart will explain or help him into or out of, I use all the intellectual elements of interpretation merely as a focal device. Unless he truly offends me, and that in which I believe (which is constantly changing in its dimensions of application, as I hope it is for everyone), I want to help him become more himself than it has been possible, so far, to be.

I want this because one of my first realizations, even in getting into this practice and teaching, is that our society, as it is presently structured, but even more so as it is presently motivated, does not give a person much of a chance to be himself in its terms. And why should he want that? Society might ask this, and my answer would be simple and the key to everything I am doing. It would be this:

"After searching your approaches for half my life, I find they are full of folly—because your recommendations benefit only those who already hold power and position and want to keep them. If this power, and these positions are benefitting people in general, I have nothing against them. But I suspect they are not and I suspect they must experience change eventually. They refuse to recognize that he is a creature of the solar system before he is a creature of any religion, city, state, nation, or political system. He was born under the stars, he lives daily with the planets of the system moving around him and, whether you prejudice him to ignore it or not, a part of him records this, becomes aware of it and moves upon it. I am saying that the world does not end at cloud level and what exists outside our cozy atmosphere is affecting our lives. No, I am saying more. I am saying that we are part of all that surrounds us and we even have a function to fulfill here on earth that has more implications than for the earth itself."

Well, that's how I'd state it. And, having stated it, I should do something about it. The first thing I had to do, as far as astrology was concerned, was to get my head out of its mind-set, because that mind-set was conceived largely by Medieval minds (and I do not mean the kind of "medievalists" Jean Sendy talks about as I explain later in this book). I am talking about the Medieval minds that were approved by the Church while it held power in Europe. It is that Church's idea of "good" and "evil" which is so interwoven into traditional astrological thinking that it might as well be an arm of the Medieval Church, though that church has passed and many of its ideas have, too.

Astrologers have also felt themselves so ostracized from the mainstream of society (and they had good reason to think this) that they have, for many years, lived in inferiority complexes (and concomitant pretensions to superiority that those complexes generated) that have boxed them into tiny worlds of thinking.

Astrology itself is so complex that these things can easily be forgotten as one plunges into the thousands of ramifications of its elements. One can become so absorbed in learning the language that he forgets what it is saying in the novelty of learning how to speak it. A lot of what astrology is saying has not been revised in any significant way since Medieval times. Yet astrologers accept it and foist it off on people who are no longer living in those times—who need an appreciation of themselves that fits the surrounds in which they now live. Well, maybe a name change will help and maybe it won't. But someday we must recognize and do something about these problems that beset us all who work with the elements of the Cosmic language.

We must examine for ourselves precisely what we are seeking to know from the language—besides learning to speak it. We must also determine what kind of view we are trying to give a person of himself through it. Do we want him to be successful? And in what terms? The terms of his own being or the terms of a society which is trying to mold him to its convenience?

If this last question were asked me, here's what I'd say: "Whenever I counsel a person I am, in the present time and circumstances, trying to advise him to be successful enough in what he is confronting, from society or himself, that he can survive to be himself on his own terms."

And I could say, for my interpretations: "I am considering that though you hope to be more, you are also still influenced by what is around you and if you are going to survive to be what you believe is your potential, then you must get through the jungle that is all around you. And, yes, my advice is often geared strongly to getting you through so you can go on to something better and more true to yourself."

Now, I must say some things about this book:

There are very few books in print that give interpretations, or even descriptions of the planets in combination. The only widely distributed one I am aware of is Reinhold Ebertin's *Combination of Stellar Influences*. It covers every planet in combination with another. But it is also written from an entirely different approach than that which someone who has studied cosmopsychology should take. And while I admire greatly Ebertin's system, and even the beauty of its logic, I am afraid I could not repeat some of those interpretations to individuals and hope to see them survive in anything but a strongly success- or failure-oriented view of living. People who want to live on that basis have my commendation of his book. But people who do not are the ones for whom the interpretation in this system are written.

It has become fashionable in astrological circles, because the whole community is hoping for an acceptance it has never yet had (and I seriously wonder whether it will be worth it to get it) to not comment on other authors' works. It is true that each one of us as an individual personality is probably unconsciously egocentered and thinks his own system is "the only valid one," but I think it is also clear that we should point out how we disagree with others in our own field. As I said, I greatly admire Ebertin and have learned much from his system, but he and I are probably not looking for the same things in a birth chart and you, the reader, should know it. I think there is room for many systems in astrology, there is room for searches for differing things. I would want none of them eliminated. But it is time we all started saying just what it is we are looking for in the cosmic mirror.

This book does not cover information on how one should fit these interpretations into an overall approach to interpretation. Other writers, basing their work on the same source (which is, in the main, the works of Dane Rudhyar), have outlined such an approach. One is Michael Meyer, the author of *A Handbook for the Humanistic Astrologer* and two others, even nearer to the approach and general search carried out here, are the authors of *The Spiral of Life*, who sign themselves as Jinni and Joanne.

The author of this book is trying to get out material on subjects that have not been covered in many other books, or at least not with the same approach. That's why this one concentrates on the subject matter it does. There are no interpretations of the planetary pairs in print yet, except in magazines, and yet they are an important element of consideration to the cosmopsychological view. Some, who follow Rudhyar and his ideas, do not like interpretations. They would rather make them for themselves. I commend them but find that most students like to have materials where they can see how someone took his own approach so they can redo it to their own search and their own method of explanation. For that reason, Chapter Five explains how I view planets when I am interpreting them in varying situations.

This is part of a series of books which will be published on the elements of interpretation. It covers only one element as thoroughly as space permits. Others in the series will follow over a period of time. They will concentrate on the subjects left out of this book that are vital to the cosmopsychological view.

Between the conception of this book and its production, a period of reflection and metamorphosis has considerably altered the original idea of what it should be. It's a replacement of a former small effort called "not a sign in the sky but a living person," yet it goes considerably beyond it. It was also meant to be a replacement of a book called *Time Out of Mind* in which the astrological elements referring to reincarnation were discussed. There was not room in this book to go into that in the way it was done before, so the original *Time Out of Mind* was reissued.

Much of the subject matter in this book deals with ideas that have come to prominence in the past few years—all of these ideas giving us a larger view of ourselves in relation to our cosmic surroundings. Astrologers should probably be aware of them, if not conversant with them. Millions of people are now intrigued with the idea that the gods of ancient times were actually spacemen who visited this planet and interfered with evolution. While the mechanical view of this might merely be a hope to identify our present mechanical kind of way of life with powers and intelligences outside us, the germ of the idea is probably leading many people to realize they do have a cosmic connection with life. That's encouraging. Astrologers often have this conception and then crunch themselves right back in the other end of the telescopic lens where they see nothing but details in aspects and houses and signs and glyphs. We also need to see clearly some of the ideas that are being used against us. But mainly, we need to look at what we are doing and question why we are doing it. Who and what for? We also need to reevaluate every element of our language in terms of its modern correlations. That's what's attempted here for at least one important element of the language.

1
Most of Us Are Asleep

Most of us are asleep while the clock of life ticks on. We stumble benumbed through a universe of mechanical days and electric nights. In our pleasures, we seek the constant Sun and try to shut the clouds from our minds. In the electronic society, few of us ever see the stars as our ancestors did or ponder, with our own senses alert to it, the fact that we are all aboard a global spaceship hurtling through the night of a galaxy even our best scientists do not yet truly understand.

We are a tiny speck in a mass of glittering lights in this galaxy—we know that—and our own Sun is the mediocre star among the luminaries. Yet we suspect we are significant, and perhaps we are.

The best minds of our generations may be like bulls stumbling through the china shop of existence when they claim to know how we human beings on the tiny planet Earth fit into the perspective of the galaxy or even the solar system.

Strangely, our archaic predecessors may have recognized the perspective better than we understand it today. Some of the minds who call themselves "scientific" are beginning, if hesitantly, to grant that possibility.

Twentieth century science is beginning to perceive in its mathematical formulae what ancient men perceived in other ways—that men on Earth are not unaffected by what happens in the skies, that patterns (more than quantities) formed "out there" have direct correlation with patterns operating in organic life on Earth.

We Have A Purpose

There are few scientists willing to admit that a moment in the sky pattern is directly analogous with the lifetime pattern of an individual human being. But many have seen the mass pattern, the pheno-monological weather pattern, the magnetic field fluctuations—and these were known once long ago, by the same ancients who extended these pattern influences from the weather to the lives of nations and kings; and, finally, in the Greek revolution of thinking, down to the individual himself.

We are asleep. But our slumber is not undisturbed. Our electronic screens show us by day the Earth spinning in a dark void of space. Our minds absorb the impressions coming from the outside. The greater mind inside begins to work on it. We may have flash perceptions in the middle of the day. Some of us let our imaginations soar with the possibilities of the vision. Others become terrified, feeling lost in a great limbo. But something happens slowly in all of us. Whether consciously or not, we absorb, once more, the great heresy to established orders of special privilege and mass ignorance: Man is a family living on a global spaceship which is spinning through the unfathomable night of a galaxy which is only one of many, many in an incomprehensible universe.

And do we, tiny as we are in that void, have a purpose within it? The ancients claimed we do. They knew of functions inside man, in their times, that psychology is bringing back to the surface today and astrologers are only now finding planetary bodies in the sky that correlate with those functions.

The ancients prophesied us. They knew a time would come when the secrets bound up in select priesthoods would be revealed to the masses. They believed this had to happen because men of this century would be forced to adopt a new level of consciousness and build a new world based upon it. They realized it could take centuries of evolution—the rise, fall, and destruction of established empires—before this stage would be reached.

But the time has arrived. Today psychology is doing publicly for the individual what the priesthood once did privately for the masses—opening up the inner skies of man. And science is doing what the priesthood once held as its exclusive province—the probing of the outer skies.

In this century, and several before, men have broken the chains of state—and church-imposed moralities that forbid the exploration of life outside us, to determine what it is rather than what we've been taught to believe it was. The results have shattered common knowledge and many who have tied their lives to it.

Now, through psychology, the same effort is being made on the biased, self-centered perceptions that are also often reinforced by church, state, and the common mentality and morality. We are reaching
inward to the cosmos inside and outward to the one surrounding our physical selves. Our material science is showing us new dimensions to the material world. But it is still mainly absorbed in the quantities and statistics of it. In science's reaction to non-statistical morality, it has forbidden itself a quest for meaning. It has offered no new moral perceptions to replace the ones it has shattered. But men seem rootless without something of that order in their lives—some kind of moral or personally guiding law to follow; some meaning to unfold in the quantities of life statistics that assail them. We are all free, nevertheless, to use what science has given us—these statistics—and apply them intelligently to a different quest in our individual lives. We can apply science's finding to our own structural quest for wholeness on the inside and on the outside of our lives.

In doing this, we must understand that there is a cosmos surrounding us. Science has shown us that. This is not a flat Earth and the personal God so many sought has not appeared to wreak vengeance on such a heresy. The skies are mute of the power that those who called on a vengeful God expected. They are mute, too, of human speech, but they can speak of vast patterns around us—to those who will comprehend a language of non-material and non-egocentered communication.

There is also a sky, or vista, inside. Psychology has begun to explore it. If all phenomenal things are accompanied by a non-phenomenal opposite (as science espouses in its perception of anti-matter and its implications), why should there not be a non-phenomenal side of man, the physical being, as well?

What's Out there Is in Us

Why should his conscious, sensory, measurable self not have an unconscious, non-sensory, immeasurable counterpart?

Here is where the cosmos does speak to man...but in the cosmos' own language, and not in man's as man's has so far developed. To those who can see or read as psychologists—and even some scientists are becoming capable of doing—the message is becoming clearer. Man is and acts within his conscious self, but all of him is not just there. And he is incapable of seeing his own eyes in themselves, much less seeing in them what stands behind them. But what is outside him is a mirror of what is in those eyes and behind them.

In the cosmos and its patterns, man can read, outside himself, what is in him and what he is involved in becoming.

This is where we drag in that old darling astrology, who has taken so many twists and turns in surviving in life that she has been called a superstitious prostitute. Once branded a prostitute, it is hard to lose the flaming scarlet letter. We must not forget the fact that no matter how she has survived, astrology has always tried to tell, man of his relation to the cosmos outside. Never mind her crudeness, her sometimes self-imposed incomprehensibility. Her fundamental reality (despite the paint and makeup) is that she has always said: "Your true function fits within a cosmic scheme—not a church, not a nation, not a city, not an ego-self; except as all these are related to the greater wholeness of which we all are part." That sounded incomprehensible to many people before our time. In such atmospheres, astrology prostituted herself in order to survive to better days.

Scientists love to bring up her prostitution rather than her fundamental reality. Psychologists have begun to see the person behind the scarlet letter. Cosmopsychology is an effort to rechristen the old darling and give her modern daughter a chance to make a new name in place of the scarlet letter.

We who practice cosmopsychology and teach it realize astrology was a prostitute. We realize, also, that she was a human entity capable of more than that and possessed of a creative depth that has been passed on to her daughter. This daughter is no longer living in a climate hostile to the idea that man is not merely involved in what goes on outside him—that he is, in profound ways, a reflection of what goes on in the skies surrounding him (a creatively willing and free, or stupidly bound, reflection of it).

But the reflection is complex; its image has many dimensions and these dimensions must be perceived clearly if we are not to remember briefly their grossest, most fleeting impressions.

The sleeper looks groggily in his mirror and catches a fleeting image. If he is engrossed in the luxury and sensuality of sleep, the reflection will show him little. It's not really that sense-arousing. The man whose eyes are not clouded and heavy, though, will look longer and deeper. The man who's awake to more than sensation will be seeking other than titillation that can arouse his tactile sense from their self-satisfied slumber.

The looker who looks and knows what he's seeking can find it even in the flashing image of a complex vision. The sleeper's unconscious takes in the same image but his awareness doesn't perceive what it contains, because he doesn't know what to look for. And he is seeking little but sensation which this reflection doesn't really contain. Only astrology as the prostitute dresses herself up for him.

There's our first step in cosmopsychology: To know what we're looking for. It isn't going to stand up and shout at us. We must be prepared to see for ourselves.

The cosmic mirror holds two important, initial dimensions for an individual to perceive. It can show him what he is, as a social being; and it can show him who he is as a social, cosmic being with a unique individual function in the evolution of his society, his culture, the whole human race and the total system to which he belongs (whether that's a family, a nation, culture, humanity, or the galaxy—he determines which).

If I were to sell you a vehicle for transportation on Earth, I'd want you to know what kind of vehicle you need to fit what you have in mind to do. That would be the first, and basic, consideration. With such basic determination made—what can the engine do?—I'd want to discuss the vehicle's other specifics. I'd want you to determine the color, the model, and its options as secondary choices.

Personality as Engine

The color, and other specifics, after all, are special options that have little to do with whether or not the engine will run and carry out the purpose you have in mind for your journey. That engine, indeed, is what will make the vehicle capable of fulfilling the basic functions to which all these unique individual considerations are appendages.

Your personality is a human engine. What was it made to do? What are its special advantages and its special quirks or limitations? What's it really suited for? Then: How do you define its operation? How do you keep it going, use it creatively, make it work practically, and stretch it beyond what the cautious man might avoid?

These are the questions we are about to ask as we approach a cosmopsychological interpretation of what you are. The answers will be found in the sky pattern that was overhead when you took your first breath of the ship's atmosphere; when you embarked upon this current life's journey through the galaxy aboard spaceship Earth. You had a role to live out on that journey—a special purpose and a unique individual function to perform on the trip. Let's see how you were made to do what will eventually make you who you are as an individual participant on the journey.

Before we go very deeply into it, however, there are some modern myths contemporary science has created about astrology that should be laid to rest. Though science generally has no truck with myths, it has been creating quite a few about some subjects it has not really thoroughly talked about, but has said just enough about that it appears the scientists know what they are saying and are saying it all. They have also created some "ideas" about astrology which they confidently and publicly attack. Unfortunately, these ideas exist nowhere but in the scientists' imagination.

2
Our God is Science Now

For many people, science is the real god of modern times. It does for them what the priesthood used to do for nations whose leader was a kind of living god on Earth. Science explores the heavens, science explains the heavens; in some people's minds, science may even be reshaping the heavens.

We probably should remember what the meaning of the word science really is, for it has become rather godly in the public mind and may one day have to suffer the sins of hubris, though its most creative spokesmen have never claimed its godliness, just its cleanliness. Still, its technicians would have one think that next to the cleanliness always stands the intimation of godliness. Here, at any rate, is a clear dictionary definition of what science, per se, means: "Any methodological activity, discipline or study." We should also remember that many individuals who were explaining science early in this century called it "the testing of rational hypotheses based on empirical data." Basically, this suggests that science is not really equipped to test the irrational or that which is not empirical. If you are not really familiar with the last word, you should understand that it means "relying on observation or experience" and "guided by experience rather than theory."

One of the men whose ideas I will next cite does not like that latter description of science's potential and he quite handily evades it by calling himself a Medieval thinker—for Medieval men believed that there was something other than experience to be guided by; that there was a tradition of revealed knowledge in mankind's early recorded experience and it was not rational as we know that term.

Myths of Science

Scientists, when they come upon the subject of astrology and decide to explain it, sound anything but rational. Many of the most creative simply do not discuss it publicly. But there are those among the technicians who like nothing better than a good punching bag. In their minds, astrology is the perfect punching bag. Sometimes it becomes a ghost, or evil spirit, to be exorcised.

One of the old wraiths that technicians always materialize (despite its slow disintegration, which becomes more obvious with the passing years) is this one: "The astrologers don't even make accurate charts any more. The signs aren't where they used to be in the sky but the astrologers persist in placing them where they were located over 2,000 years ago."

The first time a technical mind confronts one with that, he should tell the technical mind that it apparently doesn't know the difference between a sign and a constellation. A sign is a simple thirty degree section of the sky circle, which is located at a certain distance from the spring equinox point, or the beginning point of the circle. This circle is an imagined one around the Earth. It is not real. It's mathematical and it's a measuring tool projected out there into the sky. It isn't in the stars. It's in front of them from an Earth observer's point of view. It surrounds the Earth, not the stars.

This is obviously not the same as a constellation, which is a grouping of stars. A constellation is not necessarily thirty degrees in length, either, and it certainly does not coincide with the signs, or sections, of the imaginary sky circle surrounding the Earth. Remember, the sky circle is a measuring tool—a mathematical device.

The Signs Around Earth

One of the major fallacies associated with astrology is the idea that the signs of the zodiac are the constellations of stars. They are not. They are sections of a sky circle projected around the Earth. In the diagram on the next page, the ecliptic, or Sun's path around the sky, is that circle. When it crosses the equator each year, spring begins and its crossing point is the first degree of Aries. At summer solstice it reaches the Tropic of Cancer where the first degree of that sign begins. At its lowest point in the sky it touches the Tropic of Capricorn, where the beginning of that sign

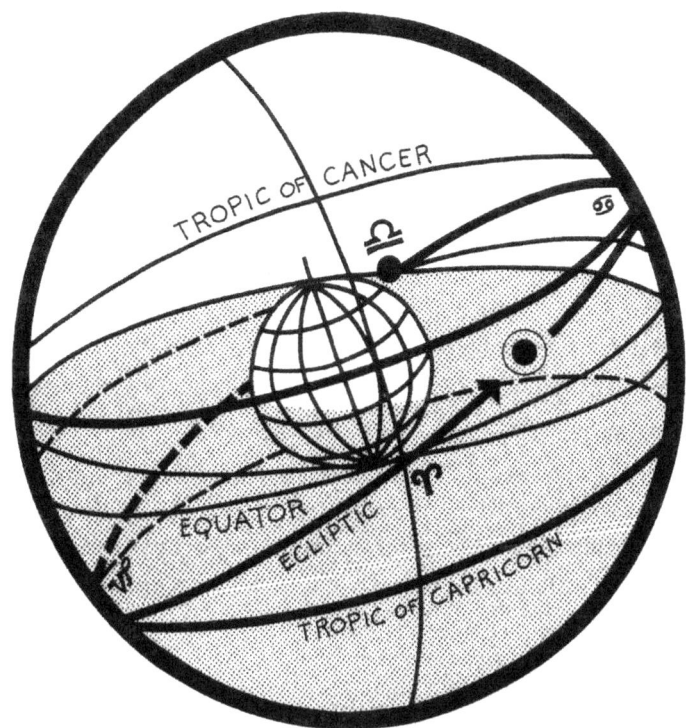

Signs Around the Earth

originates. This phenomenon of the Sun moving in its path through the sky, above and below the equator, is what creates the seasons. If you look at the diagram once again, you will see the Earth in the center of it. The screened portion of the diagram represents, on Earth, the horizon.

Look at the ecliptic again. The heavy round circle on it represents the Sun. It has a dot in its center. As you can see, when the Sun moves to the Aries point it is crossing the equator. When it reaches the Cancer point it is at its highest point above the equator. When it reaches the Libra point it will be crossing the equator again but moving south of it. At its southernmost point it is at the latitude on Earth that corresponds with the Tropic of Capricorn. In cosmopsychology we equate the zodiac with the seasons, not the stars. The stars are far off in the background. This circle, on which we project the seasonal zodiac, is around the Earth, and not in the stars. Our interpretation of the signs is seasonal in its basis, too.

Spring

When the Sun reaches the equatorial band, which is projected out into space around the Earth, day and night become equal in the northern hemisphere. If we looked out beyond the sky circle into the stars, we would probably see the early degrees of the constellation Pisces in the background—if we could see the stars in the day. We can't, of course. Astrologers and astronomers disagree on where the constellation Pisces begins and ends, so there is no agreement between them on whether the spring point (first degree of Aries) is against the constellation Pisces or against the last degrees of the constellation Aquarius.

Summer

When the Sun reaches a point above the equator equal to the Tropic of Cancer, we have the longest day of the year. The seasonal characteristics of summer are given to interpretations of the signs Cancer, Leo, and Virgo, which it passes through as it moves back toward the equator.

Fall

When the Sun comes back again to the equator, day and night again are equal. This is the beginning of Libra, from whence it moves downward with night, becoming longer and longer until finally, at Capricorn, night in the northern hemisphere is at its lengthiest.

Astrologers are very aware of the fact that the signs and the constellations to do not coincide with one another—that they have, in fact, moved apart approximately thirty degrees over a time period of more than 2,000 years. This is taken into consideration in astrological calculations.

Where astronomers and technicians themselves are ignorant is in the following knowledge: The majority of astrologers do not calculate sky charts on the basis of stars or constellations and they definitely do not interpret them on that basis. They calculate the chart according to fixed points in the sky which move backward against the backdrop of constellations, as the Earth moves through the solar system and the whole system moves through the galaxy.

In fact, as you read this book you will discover that cosmopsychology is not even interested in the stars and constellations from the point of view of their relation to the individual and his birth chart. It considers the stars and constellations relevant to cycles involving the whole planet (this spaceship on which we're all traveling together whether we realize that fact or not). To interpret the individual, cosmopsychology is not interested even in phenomena in the sky. It is interested in the patterns surrounding those phenomena. It is the patterns that have the most similarity to the individual and not the phenomena themselves.

It would be patently foolish, for instance, to say that an individual resembles the planet Mars (despite the fact that many dim-minded astrologers keep repeating that claptrap). It would be correct from our point of view, however, to say that an individual has a function operating in him that resembles the function of the planet Mars within the pattern of the solar system. It is the pattern we are observing, not Mars the planet. This latter observation is rightly left to astronomers.

In this cosmopsychological system we do not even characterize the meaning of the signs by the myths that have been spun around the stars and constellations. The meaning of signs has nothing to do with the stars. Their meaning is based on the seasons of Earth's year; the seasons that are created as the Sun moves through the sectors of the sky we have located on the mathematical circle of signs. Now, a scientist who claims that the seasons can have no effect on an individual must be practicing science on some other planet. And if a scientist is really correct in saying the signs have moved backward, he should be asked why the seasons, which coincide with the signs, have not also moved backward.

We are practicing cosmopsychology here on Earth and a fundamental tenet of our system is that the seasons, not the stars, have a direct effect upon an individual's life. We are saying that recurring patterns in the sky accompany weather on Earth and that patterns in the sky also accompany weather in the psyche of an individual human being.

Patterns Are Important

It is not the phenomena out there in the sky that interests us as much as the pattern of phenomena in people that correlates with the patterns surrounding sky phenomena.

But let us proceed to "scientific" argument No. 2 against astrology.

This is the one where the technician declares the birth chart invalid because the Earth is not included in it. As a matter of fact, though, it is. It's right there in the center of the map.

A grade school child informed that a circle like the horoscope is an abstract diagram of the sky surrounding the Earth could see that quite clearly. But a scientist wrapped up in his own special mythology might not. He is often myopic when it comes to any other view of the sky but one his own discipline currently enshrines as orthodox.

Scientific writer Jean Sendy has pointed this out quite well in a book he has written which fits onto the popular bookstands in the section where all of Eric von Daniken's sky spectaculars are featured (*Chariots of the Gods, The Gold of the Gods*, etc.). Monsieur Sendy claims there are two kinds of scientific thinking: Medieval and humanist. He calls himself a Medieval thinker because Medieval men believed in a tradition that claimed the gods once walked among men and interfered with the natural course of planetary evolution. This thought pattern was wiped out ruthlessly with the advent of the Renaissance and humanist (or evolution-centered, man-, not God-, centered thinking).

The Medievalists claimed that men didn't discover anything important—it was revealed to them by the gods. Of course Sendy believes these gods were spacemen, although he calls them Galaxians and postulates their origin as being near the center of the galaxy in the constellation Sagittarius.

Monsieur Sendy, in fact, drags up astrology to support his thesis that Earth has now entered the Age of Aquarius, when men will renew their contract with the ancient tradition and all humanists who have not been roasted alive by his words will fall over in fits of apoplexy. One supposes Sendy thinks horoscope makers will, too, but he will find that some astrologers calling themselves cosmobiologists are just as interested in the center of the galaxy as he is. In fact, they claim the galaxial center is now moving in the area of Sagittarius and interpret its significance in the birth chart as a dynamic point of influence.

Humanists, as Sendy represents them, believe men evolved to where they now stand with no help from the sky.

(For all those who have wondered why I've never strongly called my practice of astrology humanistic, here is the reason. I've long had the premonition that scientists might someday turn against the orthodoxy of evolution, and here comes Monsieur Sendy, right on schedule and probably half right in what he is saying, calling evolutionists by their Medieval name of humanists. Even Dane Rudhyar has written at times that connotations of the word humanistic may be unfortunate, considering what those following his astrological theories are really doing.)

Sendy cannot help tweaking astrology's nose, even after using one of its "ancient" traditions. He calls it the realm of "horoscope makers" and chides the ignorant fools for not including Earth in their sky maps. Now that men have gone to the Moon, he asks, what will astrologers do when the first child is born on the Moon?

I wonder what Sendy will do when the first astrologer sets up shop on the Moon. That astrologer will probably have a different ephemeris and a different tables of houses and he probably will place Earth in a horoscope calculated from the Moon's surface. It would only be logical to do. After all, Earth would be an object in the Moon's sky pattern and a rather dominant one. A rather dominant one, indeed, if you look at it realistically. For no child could be born in the Moon's atmosphere as we know it. He would die with his first breath unless he were living in an artificial Earth atmosphere transplanted to the Moon.

Such a birth would not be a real lunar birth. It would be a terrestrially-atmosphered birth, carried out on the Moon. For being a cogent thinker, Sendy seems to ignore quite a few relevant facts. I'd like to see him place Earth in his own sky while he's still standing on it.

The Spring Point

Perhaps Sendy could do that if his postulate Galaxians would once more step out of the sky and interfere with Earth's current pattern of evolution. Considering what science and technology is doing to it, there may be no more fervent prayer for this than the one coming out of Earth itself.

In *The Coming of the Gods,* Sendy claims that since 1950 the Sun has been rising at the spring equinox against the constellation Aquarius. (No matter what constellation it rises against, it rises, at that time of year, in the sign, or section of the mathematical sky circle seen from Earth that we call Aries. Let's say here, once and for all, that Aries means the first thirty degrees of a circle around the Earth measured from the spring equinox point. That's all it means in astrology, technically, as a sign.)

Astronomers have never really agreed, though, on where the constellation Aquarius begins or ends in the sky. If you asked an ancient sky observer he would give you one answer, while a modern astronomer would give you another. If you could question some modern astronomers honestly, many probably would not agree with the standard positions that are in current use. This is a problem for astrologers, also. They argue even more vehemently about the constellations' boundaries. Obviously, Sendy has determined that there's final determination on where the constellation Aquarius really begins and ends. Maybe the ancients did know from knowledge given them by the Galaxian space travelers as Sendy postulates. But one wonders if Sendy himself really knows.

Cosmopsychology accepts the positioning of the Aquarius constellation that would put the spring point in its thirtieth degree about 2,060 A.D. It also believes the present period is a transition period between Pisces and Aquarius and that science has a strong role to play in the latter.

3
But We Are Waking

Whatever we believe concerning how men came to their present state of being–whether it was through divine plan or extraterrestrial intervention—it is obvious to anyone who thinks, that we've come to the point where a new kind of consciousness is evolving.

This consciousness makes us aware, often through necessity, that man is not only affected by, but is affecting, his surroundings. The proposition of all forms of astrology has always been that the total pattern of the system in effect at a person's birth shapes his own individual pattern of life. Knowing this shape, he can know his purpose in what he will do to affect his surroundings. He can then intelligently live it out, rather than stumble through it.

All we are saying that's different in cosmopsychology is that we're concerned with the phenomena in the sky, in making the determination of individual destiny, but with the patterns made by the phenomena in the sky.

We diagram a picture of the sky at one's birth. We say that pattern was not only outside him, but was taken inside him, with his first breath. All we must do, thereafter, is translate the pattern into human terms. And this is where people become all hung up in astrology. They become so fascinated with its specialized language of houses, signs, planets, and aspects that they forget they are talking or should be talking about a human being; not a map, not an object, not even a bunch of planets, but the pattern of human potential in a person.

The Chart Elements

This must be stressed at once because in cosmopsychology it is not at all important that one know the traditional astrological terminology. In fact, it might be better if he didn't.

It would be better to know this: The circular wheel of houses in a birth chart represents activities in a human life. The signs on the cusps of these houses represent needs and attitudes the individual lives out in carrying on those activities.

The planets in the birth chart represent functions and parts of the personality. Their placement in the houses represents parts naturally geared to the particular activities of that house. Their placement in signs, within those houses, represents needs and attitudes operating in those particular parts of the personality geared to the particular activities of the houses they occupy.

The distances apart of the planets on the sky circle (and we must forget the signs and see numbers when we view these distances), represent flows of energy between the parts of the personality. When these distances form particular angles (called aspects in the astrological language) they represent accented flows of energy.

All the planets, or parts of the personality, are interrelated with one another. They all work together to keep the personality functioning. But some of these planets paired together make up vital functions of the personality and they are particularly significant.

The vital functioning of an individual requires him to adopt a personality type for operation in social terms. This shows how he functions naturally and socially as a human being. This type is determined by the angular distance between Sun and Moon at birth. Sun represents basic purpose and Moon represents daily adaptation and application of the purpose.

The individual must also define himself as a social being. This definition process is determined by the angular distance between Saturn and the Moon at birth, representing analogous functions in him that are structured psychologically by parents and society. Then he must maintain himself as a social creature. This involves the functions (social expansion and mental activity) analogous to Jupiter and Mercury at birth.

The individual reproduces himself–in kind and in abstract. This involves functions (masculine and feminine drives, or desires and values) analogous to Mars and Venus at birth.

If he's going to survive in society's terms, he must operate in a practical manner. This involves functions in him (social shaping and social expansion) analogous to Saturn and Jupiter at birth.

Finally, if he is going to become an individual–that is, bring the creature society makes of him into alignment with his own inner drives for individual realization–he must stretch his operation beyond mere social satisfaction. This involves functions (social shaping and individual potential) in him that are analogous to Uranus and Saturn at birth.

The foregoing will not be learned from traditional astrology. In fact, one of its great problems is that in the haste and confusion of its twentieth century renaissance, it is still inadvertently looking at men as astrologers looked at them in the classical Medieval and Renaissance periods.

Astrology in its traditional forms is not looking at individuals at all. It is looking at mathematical representations of them in terms of quantities and social statistics, as well as social values of "good and bad." One part of us is social. We use it as a vehicle in which we become individuals. But another part of us cannot be classified successfully in social terms. We also have two levels of operation in the modern world.

One of these is conscious and controlled by the ego, which parents and society instill in us. The other is unconscious and non-ego-powered. In fact, it is often threatening to the isolation and self-satisfaction of the realm of ego-awareness. This is not surprising since parents often do not see the child within but the child they wish were within.

We Must Rebuild It

Here is where cosmopsychology differs strongly from other applied systems of astrology. It is interested in you as the individual that was the potential inside you, and not as the socially statistical type outside influences would like to see you molded into. Yet this system realizes that the social part of you does fit a typing pattern and you have to understand what that pattern is, and where it places you among others, in order to see how you differ from them as an individual. You have to see the vehicle your individuality is using in order to know what, and how, it is doing.

We must reorder almost every category and priority of traditional astrological interpretation in order to see this. Medieval astrology did not even conceive of the person as an individual, but as a vassal of the church and the community. We are no longer living in a Medieval society and we must find our bearings in modern times.

It is the time of day you were born, and the latitude and longitude at which you were born, that makes you individual. This time structured the outer wheel of your birth chart. It placed specific degrees of the zodiacal circle of development on the house cusps of the chart. It placed the planets with an axis of orientation to the space surrounding you at birth. This degree-axis-space formation is your real individuality as it wants to operate out into life. This axis formation spells out the specific function I said you were made to perform when you boarded spaceship Earth for this life's journey.

The day of the month and year you were born determined the placement of the planets in the signs and their distance apart on the sky circle. This gave you a personality type and vital functions to shape it for operation. This is the subject of this volume of cosmopsychology.

Let's say that the real you is an abstract entity that puts on a body and a psyche just as someone would get into a vehicle to make a journey. The engine and its parts would make the vehicle capable of operating in particular situations.

In essence, that's what you did when you were born. You entered a human vehicle. You should know how it operates so that later you can see why it was designed as it was to perform a specific (your birth chart axis message) function, using a general operating pattern (the planetary interrelationships, which become the engine of your destiny and not its shape, though much of the shape is due to the kind of engine it uses).

The distance apart, or the operative nature, of the vital functions of you (analogous to Sun, Moon, Mercury, Venus, Mars, Jupiter, Saturn, and Uranus in the sky) make up this engine. It has a type (Sun and Moon relationship), a defining power (Saturn/Moon relationship), maintenance power (Jupiter/Mercury relationship), reproductive power (Mars/Venus relationship), personality power (Saturn/Jupiter relationship), and individualizing power (Uranus/Saturn relationship).

In order to see all these things, one needs a birth chart calculated to the accurate time and place of birth. A birth time that's off a few minutes will not change the kind of engine one possesses (in most cases we'll see), but it will change the individuality aspects of his total nature. An astrological reading geared to some problem, question, or situation does not require an accurate chart. A rough one will often suffice. But when it comes to understanding oneself truly, an accurate birth time from which to calculate an accurate chart is a necessity. It is also better for the individual if he can come to see for himself his individuality, rather than having it "told" to him by an astrologer. It takes time to learn it and individual participation to grasp it, and this can hardly ever be accomplished in the typical astrology "reading" session. There's too much to deal with for the time allotted to such a reading. There's also a participation on the part of the individual under study that is essential to the grasp of the birth pattern's real meaning and how it has, or has not, been implemented so far in his life. The birth chart cannot tell what the individual has done so far to live out his pattern and it definitely cannot tell the specifics of the environment in which he came to live out the pattern. Yet they can have a tremendous bolstering or defeating effect upon it.

This is not generally understood, yet it should be.

This volume dwells on the significance of the distance apart of the pairs of planets on the sky circle–in reality, in a person, the energy and character of vital functions of the social personality, as well as the first steps of stretching beyond it into individual realization of oneself, both inside and outside.

Aspects Sound Fearful

In technical terms it will be necessary to see the distances apart of the planets to see how and why the vital functions operate as they do. It will also be necessary to perform calculations involving the Ascendant, or rising degree, to see where these vital functions seek outlets through individualized activity (where they operate in the houses of the chart as they make their way out through the Ascendant, which represents this lifetime's real individuality).

There is an abstract measuring cycle that will be applied to determine the how and why of the operation of the vital functions. It is based on the monthly lunation (or Sun/Moon relationship) cycle. But it applies to the energy flow between any two planets or bodies moving in the sky (which represents parts of the personality operating in the individual). This cycle's pattern stands behind all operations in the human being which require an expenditure of energy.

This cycle has eight phases–each with a special purpose and characteristic type of action–based on the distance apart of the bodies on the sky circle. All of astrology's traditional aspects operate within the cycle and its phases. They cannot be seen clearly until one visualizes them within the cycle. This is because the aspects are only accentuations of energy within each phase and step of the overall energy distribution cycle. They do not, and cannot, operate outside it. The lack of knowledge on the latter observation is one of the major failures of traditional astrology.

Practitioners of the tradition have made the aspects sound so horrifying that the novice coming to the textbooks can be frightened out of his wits quite easily by their interpretations. He is hardly ever told that one aspect leads to another and the dynamic ones set up situations in which the so-called easy ones can operate. Tradition doesn't see the wholeness in which the cycle operates.

4

To A New Vision

A person who has lived life within "respectable" social constructs and wants to continue doing so will probably find all he wants to know about himself in traditional astrology. It is geared almost entirely to such a person.

A person who wants to know how he can live with a purpose beyond this—the purpose of actualizing his own potential no matter what's respectable (and it changes rather frequently)—will probably not find what he's looking for in traditional astrology. Astrology, in the majority, is seeking acceptance into the respectable world and has molded itself according to the conventions operating there (and since the conventions change so rapidly now, it is easy to see the reasons for some of astrology's schizophrenia and abrupt about-faces). The abstracts of astrology, however, do not change no matter how much the social climate does. So Mr. and Mrs. Normal are merely getting translated versions of themselves from traditional astrology.

Still, however, there are some strange things about a conventional person which even he knows deeply within, that it may seem to him traditional astrology passes over or misses in its view of him. Some of what is missed will be found immediately in cosmopsychology.

A Specific Example

An outstanding specific example of what the tradition would miss would be found in the makeup of an individual who was born, let us say, when three or four sky bodies were rising in Capricorn and at such a time of the day that the Sun and Moon would also be there, with the Moon several degrees ahead of the Sun in the zodiac.

Traditional astrology would probably describe this person as ambitious, prudent, calculating and, perhaps, austere in his approach to others.

How would it be able to explain to itself that despite the presence of those nuances in his attitudes, he is, in operation, a spontaneous magnetic person—an individual who wishes to plunge into activity without knowing where it's going but with the confidence in himself that he will find out as it moves along and manage it on the spur of the moment. That's hardly austere or calculating.

Tradition in astrology simply wouldn't be able to describe this facet of his personality in operation. Yet his friends would be very aware of it. Some of them would probably call him a star, a real personality, and an individual possessing a kind of charm or charisma. They would be aware he operates in anything but a traditional Capricorn manner. His purpose, inside, might be Capricorn in nature, but the personality in which he deals with people would often be more aptly described in the traditional manner of Leo!

Richard Nixon, thirty-seventh president of the United States, was a similar kind of personality (though his planetary sign positions were not the same as those cited in the foregoing example; but Sun and Moon were in the same phase of the lunation cycle). He needed crowds for assurance, and he projected a strange kind of charisma to them. The austerity, the aloofness were there. But his mode of operation could hardly be described in terms of Capricorn. He plunged into activity. He changed courses in mid-stream. He declared one principle this month and another precisely the opposite the following month. He seemed to be living in the moment and did what was expedient to the moment. The latter was undoubtedly his major downfall. But all of this was natural to him—even acting his way through.

The reason for this is that though the Sun was in Capricorn at his birth, he was very different from other personalities born with the same Sun sign position. His personality, apart from any sign consideration, was New Moon, or what I call the leader-performer. His engine of destiny gave him a human vehicle that operated more like Leo than like Capricorn.

Traditional astrology never did correctly assess the personality of this president because it never saw it in astrological terms.

The reason why he, or any other Capricorn with the Moon located from zero to forty-five degrees ahead of the Sun at birth, is different is quite simple. There are eight kinds of personalities that can be born when the Sun is in Capricorn. There are eight kinds of personalities that can be born when the Sun is in any sign of the zodiac. They all have the same basic sign purpose, but they don't operate as the purpose. They operate as the personality type equips them. This is because there is a lunation or New Moon every thirty days. It takes the Sun about thirty days to move through a sign of the zodiac. But while it is doing this, the Moon moves through all twelve of the signs and makes eight phases or dynamic aspects with the Sun while it is moving from one lunation to the next.

The Capricorn purpose is operative in all these personalities if the Sun is in Capricorn when they're born, but each one of them has a different way of applying that purpose into life on a daily basis (each one has the possibility of having the Moon at his birth located in one of eight different dynamic relationships to the Sun).

This is where cosmopsychology differs dramatically from the tradition. We don't want to simply add up all the parts of the personality. We want to see the interplay of action and energy between them because psychologically this action pattern is a powerful key to assessing the individual. We try to see how the personality's parts are structured to operate with one another, no matter what each part appears to be when examined on its own and apart from the rest. This latter method of seeing is an extremely deceptive one. You could look at a man's hand in repose and see quite a lot about it. If you assess it on what you've seen at its rest, you'll miss quite a lot. You will never know its natural mode of operation until you see it put into action or to work. Putting it to work requires the individual's brain to instruct it to move. As soon as the brain does this, we have more than the hand itself operating. We have some of the total individual's motives and some of his training guiding that hand. Their relationship to it can make it operate entirely differently from the way it would if it were on its own.

The preceding is true of every part of our personalities. No one part operates separately or singly. Each one operates in cooperation with another. We can see them at rest for what they are individually, but we can't see them in action until we see how they were structured to operate together. This has nothing to do with signs.

The Key to Operation

The direction of one part often determines the shaping of the other. One part may be constructed admirably to operate along certain lines but it must operate in cooperation with another part which is directing its actions. This is what we try to see that is not yet incorporated into the tradition as it is operating in the modern world.

In order to see this, we must understand a cycle of energy distribution that operates in all planetary cycles (and in all vital human functions) irrespective of the planets' placement in the signs (and irrespective of the separate structure of each part which makes up one-half of the vital function).

This cycle is the key to operation of the personality and not to the shape of its parts. That's why this book is called The Engine of Destiny.

The cycle is based on a phenomenon men have watched in the sky since the Moon orbited the Earth. They have watched its dynamics unfold with the increasing and waning light that moves over the Moon's face every month. They have seen the tides of the ocean move in rhythm to it and they have felt the tides of emotion and reaction build and subside with it in themselves.

What we have discovered in cosmopsychology is that it doesn't have to be visible to the eye to be present and operative. The nature of the cycle is present in the cyclic motion between any two bodies moving on the sky circle.

The implications of its nature are present in any two parts of the personality when they operate together to make up a human function. They're particularly noticeable in the dynamic functions.

This is not only true in basic makeup (where we extract a moment out of the sky's motion and say its pattern is you). It is true as well in the cycles of energy thrown at the person from outside influences (represented in transits) and in the cycles of energy that well up from inside and try to influence development of the basic makeup (primary and secondary directions) as it unfolds into life on an individual time schedule.

As you will soon see, it is necessary to understand, because of this cycle's operation, that there are two kinds of every aspect used in traditional astrology.

One of them is instinctive and spontaneous in nature, often leading to unplanned action. Another is conscious and controllable.

It is necessary to see that no aspect ever operates before the one that has preceded it or after the one that follows it. One aspect follows another in an order that is knowable in advance. In other words, aspects cannot be extracted from this cycle. They are structured by it and their meaning and purpose are determined within it.

Let's look at the cycle.

Any two bodies we can see moving in the sky have at some time been in the same location on the sky circle. They will, at some point, be opposite one another on it, and they will eventually move back together on it This may not happen in the same sector of the sky (that is, the same sign), but it will happen. All of this occurs because one body moves faster than the other and yet both are moving along the circle. So they come together, they separate and oppose one another, and then they come together again. All that varies, with different pairs of objects under consideration, is the time that elapses as the cycle forms, unfolds, and reforms.

With some bodies the cycle operates monthly, with others, it takes years, and for some, it takes more than a century. But all of them go through the cycle with one another and we call it the cycle of relationship.

It shows how energy flows from one part to another and it shows how vital functions are structured to operate together in making parts of the personality become more than what they appear to be when considered separately. The slower moving body is the reference point of the cycle. We locate it first and then determine the faster one's distance from it to discover what phase of the cycle is in effect between them. We see the slower body as shaping, or determining, action and the faster body as carrying it out according to the fundamental purpose of the slower one. One is distributing what the other has conditioned. They can operate separately in some things, but not in the vital functions of keeping the personality in operation.

Instinct and Control

After the two come together in the sky circle, the faster one moves ahead of it to make an opposition. This is the instinctive, uncontrolled part of the cycle when activity is unconsciously motivated and precipitated. It is the part of the cycle, too, in which structures are built before they are used, before they are given content or meaning.

When the faster body has made the opposition to the slower, it then moves behind it on the sky circle to catch up with their next meeting point. This is the considered part of the cycle when action can be consciously controlled, or intelligently manipulated. It is also the time when structures built under the previous half of the cycle are found inadequate and abandoned, or are given meaning and used purposefully and consciously.

This latter is the controlled climax and reward side of a cycle that was begun with instinctive self-structuring and self-expression that was planned consciously inside at the end of a previous cycle but could only manifest after the beginning of the current one.

This is the cycle. It applies to any two bodies in motion in the sky. It applies to any two parts of the personality (which planets, Sun, and Moon represent) when they operate together to make up the vital functions of the personality. The personality is the individual's vehicle of operation in society, and if he is going to make his journey successfully through it and all the conditions he will encounter in it, this vehicle must function.

I doubt whether an intelligent person would take a sports car on a trip to the Arctic. There would be a vehicle suitable to such a trip. The inherent logic of the birth moment is that it occurred when there was a vehicle coming to life that would suit the purpose of the individual's role, or function, in life (shown in the axis of the chart).

5

Reading the Cycle in Lives

The diagram below is an abstract picture of the lunation cycle being used as a basis of interpretation in this book. On the wheel appear all the major aspects used in astrology, yet they are found within overriding groupings called phases of the cycle. Each phase begins with a hard, or dynamic, aspect, for these aspects, even in astrology's traditional interpretation, are the ones that initiate action in life. Within each phase, which covers forty-five degrees of the circle, are contained all the softer aspects traditionally used by astrologers. The contention of cosmopsychology is that the hard aspects have more powerful ramifications than the softer ones. They initiate flows of energy that lead to other, less powerful, uses of the same energy.

The Phases of Activity

All aspects within the forty-five degree span, or phase, are conditioned by the overall impetus given at the opening of the phase. Thus, we see all the aspects of astrology operating within a cycle, each one following another that makes way for it, or sets up energy that it can use. This negates some of the negative qualities attributed to individual aspects because each aspect, as seen within this cycle, has some definite purpose to carry out. That purpose is the meaning of the phase of the cycle. For instance, all conjunctions (when two planets meet at zero degrees apart) initiate projection of some idea, some impulse, some project, or some activity. There follows, after the conjunction, a thirty degree aspect, which is traditionally called either mildly benefic or irritating. Why is either term used? What reason do astrologers give? If they can't give one, this system can.

Reading the Cycle in Lives

Whatever irritation or even mild benefit that would come from use of energy at the thirty degree aspect after conjunction would be because two planets (which could be compatible or antithetical in nature) merged their energies at conjunction. Following this they moved into the thirty degree alignment in which the energy had to flow in a different manner. Thirty degrees, by sign, or by house, represents two different kinds of activities. They are often polar in nature, but one follows the other as well when an overall cycle of activity or attitude and need (which signs represent) is considered. Therefore, the thirty degree aspect represents a polarity, or combination, of planetary energy merging—and this can be mildly beneficial (because it takes a great deal of effort to make two antithetical energies work together, in many cases) or irritating (for the same reason).

But there is a purpose behind this which is never mentioned in traditional interpretation. That purpose, after the conjunction, is for projection of something new. The impulse is there at the conjunction. The polarities must be merged, if it's going to work, at the semisextile.

And if they are merged well, there follows a thirty-six degree aspect which represents, at least to some astrologers, "an instinctive kind of style in attempting to create." Wouldn't that logically follow if two polarities were merged in order to project something?

After this meeting, merging, and evolution of personal style, the next aspect is the forty-five degree dynamic flow of energy which initiates another phase of activity. After projection comes the struggle forward from it. A forty-five degree aspect represents mobilization forward. Forward from what? From the past which existed before the meeting. It must be broken if the future suggested by the meeting is to materialize.

Within this crescent phase opened by the forty-five degree aspect, we follow with the fifty-one degree, twenty-six minute aspect (fate, as Marc Edmund Jones referred to it), the sixty degree aspect, and then the seventy-two degree aspect. If the two polarities cannot work together when a mobilization is required, something had better interfere with this cycle. That is what we consider to be the fate of the fifty-one degree, twenty-six minute aspect. If the cycle is getting nowhere, fate may inter-

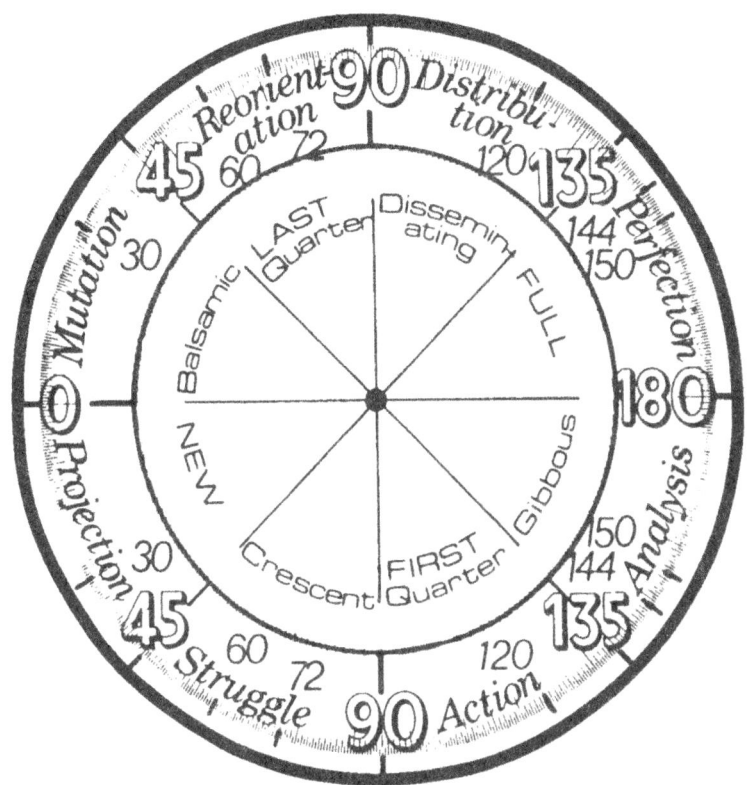

Reading the Cycle in Lives

cede to stop it or throw it for a loop that will repolarize it. Once this is done, the mobilization can proceed productively (the meaning of a sixty degree aspect) if an effort is put into it and finally creatively (the meaning of the seventy-two degree aspect). The aspects operate in a similar fashion throughout the 360 degree cycle (which is split into two 180 degree hemispheres, one representing conscious action and one representing instinctive action) with all aspects, in the same order, but backwards, repeating themselves after the opposition point, or 180 degree mark.

We can use this cycle and make sense of it in the birth combinations of planets; in transits; in secondary progressions; and even in primary or solar arc directions. All we have to do, in considering the combination of two planets within this cycle, is know which is the reference point and which is moving in relation to that reference point. Since both are moving and keep moving, no sign or degree of sign can be the reference point for longer than one moment. We must only use the sign positions to measure distance apart on the 360 degree wheel to determine how they stand in relation to one another. This is very simple in the birth chart because the planets are static once they are extracted from the sky. That's what a birth chart is: A static representative of one moment in the sky which once existed, but passed and exists now in microcosmic form in the person whom the birth chart represents. That is why we call a person's birth chart one moment of time or the sky's representative on Earth.

Applying It Technically

When we consider a birth chart, finding the reference point is simple.

All planets move at differing speeds in the sky. One is faster in motion than the other. The slower one becomes the reference point. The faster one is either ahead of it after the conjunction has been made or behind it after the opposition has been made.

If the birth chart is plotted on a continental chart form (a true circle with 360 degrees on it so one can place the planets at their proper distance apart on it), the wheel can be used to see immediately what phase of the cycle any two planets would fall into in relation to one another. One would simply point the zero of the wheel at the slower of the two planets (by sky motion) and note where, along the wheel and in the phases or near what aspects, the faster one was located. This would be done the same with secondary progressions. But both progressed planets would be used rather than a birth planet to a progressed planet. (One could do this if any birth planet were considered static, or slower, because it doesn't move from its birth place if one is considering it at its birth place.)

With transits we merely consider the birth planet as the reference point. It is static (it remains in the natal chart at the same degree all one's life) while all transiting planets are moving. With primary progressions it is much the same. One birth planet is static in relation to the movement of a directed planet no matter how their normal motion in the ordinary sky differs.

All we have to do then is interpret the abstracts of this cycle into the basic meaning of whatever combination of planets we are considering. Only the vital functions of the personality are considered in this text. But theoretically, the cycle could be applied to any two planets if we realized what they meant in the person. That is most people's problem in astrology—determining what the planets mean as parts of the personality. Because of that I have in this text written out interpretations rather than elaborating upon the cycle itself. Each pair of vital functions is considered here, phase by phase. If someone else wrote interpretations, they might differ because that person might have other nuances of meaning for what Venus or Mars represents in the personality. The basic cycle is explained exhaustively in *The Transit of Saturn* and is here applied, by interpretation, to basic planetary pairs.

For those who want to penetrate the reasoning behind the interpretations, the following are basic considerations in applying the meaning of birth planetary pairs.

Sun/Moon

The Sun is the conscious purpose of existence and the Moon is the manner of acting it out in daily activity. There are no objects brighter in the Earth's sky than Sun and Moon. Therefore, they are taken as the key to -personality type. They were always called the lights by astrologers. How about lights of the life? Sun can be interpreted as aim, goal, vitality, or any number of human functions including conscious purpose, conscious goal, self-orientation, or central awareness, and central personal drives. Moon can be interpreted as habits, mannerisms, responses to others. Sometimes I call it your ability to be adaptable to changing situations. When I think of it negatively, I think of it as habits hanging over the person from the past (from past lives as well) and inflexibility in situations that demand change.

Saturn/Moon

Saturn represents the boundaries of the conscious awareness. It also represents what you are taught by society and what is drilled into you by the authority figure in your early family life—usually the father. It represents parental shaping in your life. The father gives you his name. The Moon in this combination represents the habits you were taught to live out that name. I also think of it as youthful conditioning. This is a psychological pair (or human function) that gives you an identity on society's record. You have a name and you give it a reputation by the habits you've been taught because people associate what you do when you're young with the name they call you. If you don't believe that, think back to the Jones kid in your neighborhood. Your reaction to the word Jones is probably conditioned by him. If he always had a runny nose and you thought him uncouth, perhaps you should consider whether his mother (Moon) taught him how to use a handkerchief so his peers wouldn't think of his nature (Saturn) as that of a kid with a runny nose.

Jupiter/Mercury

Jupiter represents your ability to reach out for what you need to exist. It also represents optimism, good luck, morality, and religious leanings. Psychologically, however, it is the outreaching part of you that tries to make its way in society. Once you want to impress yourself on someone else you start talking. That brings in Mercury, which is your sensory ability to assimilate the results (impressions) of your contacts with your surroundings. I call it your communicating mechanism because just about every contact you make outside yourself requires communication. You also write, speak, and move around. These two are the key to all those activities. But they are also your moral leanings or teachings (Jupiter), thus bringing in religion and your early and formal, or public, education (Mercury)—for that's where you developed your mentality.

Planets as Functions

Mars/Venus

Mars is your animal energy, your physical aggressiveness, your sexual drive, and your personal desires. Venus is your softer side, your personal sociability, your personal values, and your receptivity to another on a one-to-one basis. We could call Mars your masculine side and Venus your feminine side if you will realize everyone has both. If you were all masculine, you'd probably never rest, and if you were all feminine, you might never move. Mars initiates. Venus receives. Venus also wants, but Mars goes out to get what Venus wants. What if Mars doesn't like what Venus wants and grabs onto something else? That's what half the interpretations are about because the two, in about half the people, do not agree on what's desirable.

Nevertheless, they have to work together. There's one Mars and one Venus in every sky. They're creativity as well as love and sex.

Saturn/Jupiter

Saturn, because of parental and societal conditioning, represents your conservative streak—the thing that tells you you can have so much and no more. This is conditioned by your father's name and place in society (don't tell me John Kennedy would have been president in the 1960s if he'd been African-American and born in Harlem). Jupiter represents your urge to expand this, to make it greater, bigger, more productive. Jupiter is your urge to expand and Saturn is your sense of reality in terms of the times in which you live and the society in which you operate. Thus, together I call them your sense of practicality and making it in economic terms.

Uranus/Saturn

Uranus is the spiritual voice inside that tells you society doesn't know everything; that you can be an individual beyond its terms. Saturn is the voice of society. They're in conflict, but it's this conflict between static structure (Saturn) and fledgling genius or creativity (Uranus) that makes individuation possible. There are a number of other valid concepts here for the Saturn and Uranus combination. You could say that Saturn is your worldly father speaking to you, or commanding you, in distinction to Uranus, being your cosmic father trying to speak to you. There is also the necessary comprehension that one of these voices is controlling your sensory world of being (Saturn) and the other is not (Uranus), but as soon as you get out of that sensory world (that is, go to sleep, or drift off into daydreams or periods of inspiration) the non-worldly father gets his chance.

This is why I call it the individuation "process" rather than "function." The functions of the personality are controlled, and conscious and unconscious (and often in conflict when the conscious fears what is greater than it) do not. Only one-half of them does. And it is the conscious (Saturn) that can choose to listen to the unconscious and follow it (thus, often destroying its own stability in the conscious, or predictable, world) or try to ignore it. The conscious, however, cannot shut up the unconscious. And every time it tries to escape in its own world what it does not want to handle or becomes too lazy to handle (in some cases), it is opening itself up to this world of the unconscious.

Now, let's look in abstract at what happens through the cycle of relationship. And see it geared to the personality. The personality is made up of pieces taken out of a whole cycle. One person represents a piece, here and there, of different whole cycles which affect groups of people when they're happening, but condition individuals when they breathe them in and are shaped by them. A function of your personality may be operating in one phase of the cycle all your life (because the birth planets do not change, or it would be like having your bones change position from their basic interrelationship during your lifetime—they may change in small ways but not in basic structure). But there is another person who is born just before you, and one after you, who has the same function operating in the phase before yours or the phase after. This is how you belong to a whole of people. You represent one aspect of it—perhaps the difficulty (ninety degree aspect within a personality function) that makes possible a condition of ease (120 degree aspect which follows it)—and the other person represents another. So you're not unconnected to others. You may be initiating, through one facet of your personality, something that another personality around you may have to carry out, or let's say can only carry out because you made it possible.

Operating in Wholeness

New Phase

Anything here has the power of instinctive projection. It follows impulse. It radiates charm. It is spontaneous and operates best without a plan or contrivance. The thirty degree aspect indicates difficulty in bringing two polarities together. Thirty-six degrees shows a personal technique has been employed to make them work together.

Crescent Phase

This begins at forty-five degrees, and is a mobilization forward from the merging of the two planets or functions. They must move ahead to break from the past (a cycle culminated before the conjunction). This becomes productive at sixty degrees, personally creative at seventy-two degrees.

First Quarter Moon

The mobilization has operated; this precipitates a crisis in the surroundings at ninety degrees. This can be a battle or a need to clear the surroundings of obstacles. Aggressive action. If it succeeds, forward movement resumes easily at 120 degrees. One can drift or move swiftly.

Gibbous Phase

After action, it's time to analyze what kind of action would create less waste or friction in the future. This may take a period of apprenticeship in the surroundings because they are challenging (the 135 degree aspect). If this succeeds, technical competence sets in (144 degrees) but one can get lost in techniques; he needs to learn to be flexible (150 degrees).

Full Phase

Flexibility is important because the movement on instinct has accomplished a structure, way, or pattern. It's been battling its way through. Now it must receive content, meaning, or direction (180 degrees), receiving what it is not by instinct. There can be an avoidance (150 degrees) of this necessity, but if accepted the individual is now skilled in a conscious way (144 degrees) and he is ready to go into the disseminating phase.

Disseminating Phase

In the disseminating phase he challenges his surroundings with what he has learned (135 degrees) and moves creatively (120 degrees) to what he believes. This is the purpose of the whole cycle. Its apex is here.

Last Quarter

What's done is done. Now there's another challenge, from inside (90 degrees), to become aware of a distant future and begin moving productively (60 degrees) or creatively (72 degrees) toward it by choice.

Balsamic

If this is accomplished, there is a mobilization toward the future inside. The old body (psychological or physical) is ill-equipped for what's ahead. The consciousness must find a creative technique (36 degrees) for merging itself with the spirit of a latent new body of activity and this may not be easy (30 degrees) to merge two polarities but it must be done so the future can live anew (zero to conjunction of new cycle).

6
The Planets in Pairs

Whenever we interpret something and fix it in terms of the present, we tend to limit it. That is the great problem that forever confronts us in dealing with things across time. As Plato tried to show the Western world, it is the forms from which all things spring, and each limited thing is but an imperfect manifestation of the form which covers, in its purity (I'd rather say comprehension), all possible forms of the same function.

It is impossible when interpreting astrology, or any other language to stick to the pure form and ignore the language of the moment. Unfortunately, that momentary language is what people are speaking and what they understand. It would be like speaking Latin to Italians or undeviatingly correct English to Americans. You might win intellectual honors but you might also never be understood and if your urge is to communicate, you had probably better do what is required to get your idea across, particularly if you're trying to help someone, no matter how impure his grammar is.

The Engine in Words

The above argument does not, of course, suggest that one should plunge into the colloquial language and reshape himself. If he has something to say, it's likely to come through on some middle ground.

The language in which the following interpretations are written is a kind of blend of popular psychology (that is, not academic), diluted technical astrology, and what I hope is a strange kind of common sense.

The reader will have to determine for himself. It's my contention in trying to build a contemporary astrological language through cosmopsychology that the language changes outside astrology and its application should try to follow it, though not necessarily wallow in it so much that it loses its own integrity. I've tried to give the abstracts of my reasoning so that the questioning person can contradict, for himself, what he finds wrong or misstated here. I would like to see people who learn the astrological abstracts apply them to their own lives in their own unique ways. But sometimes, I suppose, they need to see how someone else did it for himself. Well, this is how I'd do it.

There is a small technical thing to say about it. I have found from my own experience that the phase, in personality functions, does not begin to be valid until the actual aspect is formed. It is then valid in the sky for any person or persons born under it until the next aspect is exact. In other words, there is no orb of phase, only orb of aspect. A phase is in effect until the next one is exactly formed. And each phase begins on a dynamic aspect which is zero or a multiple of forty-five as the big numbers on the diagram in Chapter 5 show. That's my finding; someone else might discover something different.

One final note: I have skipped some aspects under some functions because they didn't seem to be that important in interpretation. The functions are grouped by phase. This is as thorough as I can be on a subject that has never been published in interpretation form before.

Performer
Actor, Leader, Instigator

New Moon:

Moon at birth is zero to forty-five degrees ahead of the Sun.

Center stage, with no script, and only your wits and instincts to follow is the most likely place for you to be found in life. You're an impetuous, spontaneous type of individual and you're best when you meet life head on, rather than trying to plan carefully for it.

You function well in crisis and you're able to draw others to you for support because whatever else you do, you also radiate a kind of human warmth which becomes, over a period of time (no matter what sign the Sun was in at birth, and some are described as cold and withdrawn), a kind of charisma you are capable of broadcasting like a vulnerable appeal for help. It does you no good to plan a thing out in detail; in the final analysis you're likely to contradict every step of any plan you have announced because the instinct of the moment told you you could get better results by improvising.

Your conscious aims (the Sun's sign) and your responses to life around you (the Moon's sign) are galvanized for action together. It does you no good to be deceptive because your very mannerisms (Moon) make your aims (Sun) transparent. You are, in most cases, what you appear to be. But you are also whatever the situation demands. That's your great asset. There's no better personality to plunge right into a problem and see it through to a conclusion without knowing in advance what the end result will be.

People have to believe in the essential you, because they will never be able to predict, except in very general terms, what you will be today on the basis of what you said or did yesterday. Life is a stage to you and if you have the inner goal of making your role as productive for others as it is for yourself, you will deserve the billing you're certain to get.

You have one great problem. You can stand in your own ego and cast shadows where you would rather spread light. This is most likely to happen when you insist that your way is the only way. That simply doesn't make sense when you actually examine it. The method you used yesterday is probably not the one you'll use today or the one you'll adopt tomorrow. Your goal may be the same, but your method is expediency. It fits only the situation and it's as changeable as the wind because you do what will work.

You were meant to lead and people will probably follow but you'll be remembered better in the end if you lead them to what will make them greater individuals rather than what would make you a greater name. Whatever you do, though (and this will be your own great test), they're not likely to forget you.

30°

Moon is within orb of a thirty degree aspect of the Sun while still being ahead of it.

You're the same as other New Moon personalities with one exception. Your habit patterns and your aims are often out of step with one another. Sometimes you have to make enormous efforts to bring them together. This means that you sometimes respond to people, out of habit, in ways that don't seem to fit your basic aims.

You still don't have to think about the techniques of any specific situation, but you have to analyze what you're doing, in general, by habit; that often seems to distract you from your goals. You have to try to learn to bring the two together. Either your habits are ill fitting to what you've announced you're aiming for or your aims are being sabotaged by your inflexibility to new situations. This can cause you to appear or actually be deceptive, and this will not fit with the trust that people have placed in you.

36°

Moon is within orb of a thirty-six degree aspect of the Sun, while ahead of it.

Your special uniqueness of New Moon personality is that people are likely to remember the personal touches you leave on a situation. This is because you are technically adept and there are styles and nuances you bring to every situation–gestures that mark them as yours. You're likely to be memorable for style.

Saturn/Moon in New Phase

Moon is zero to forty-five degrees ahead of Saturn.

You may have felt tremendously disciplined by parental or authority figures in your early life. You don't need to think consciously about projecting an identity. You have one that's almost automatic. It is so strong, in fact, that you may seem overwhelmed by it. But strangely enough, even the pressure you feel under gives you a kind of human charm that radiates forth from you.

The difficult part of this is that in the second part of your life (from ages twenty-eight through fifty-six) it may be difficult to break out of the identity patterns you were forced into when you were young. What you will have to do is seek some pattern in which to mold yourself that will be easy to follow. Again, you'll probably find it without much trouble. You are very much what you appear to be, but it is shaped powerfully by whatever you follow or believe in. Remember that. What you believe is what you become. You can hardly avoid it. Choose your beliefs carefully because once you've adopted them, you'll follow them spontaneously–

and that's about your only way because you are what you give your allegiance to.

Jupiter/Mercury in New Phase
Mercury is zero to forty-five degrees ahead of Jupiter.

You're the spontaneous talker, writer, teacher, or communicator. You work best on the spur of the moment and without a script. You can sense what an audience needs and you hold it within yourself to give if you find you believe enough in a thing that you will let it come forth from you without contrivance or plan. When talking, you can virtually hypnotize people because it isn't the ego speaking in you so much as it is the basic beliefs you hold (Jupiter) pouring out through your social communication mechanism (Mercury).

You need an audience, but you also need something to believe in that the audience needs to hear or understand. Your charm is in your communication of what you believe or understand. Make it broad and make it deep. But never contrive it. Express it as it wants to come forth and you won't go far wrong with it. If you're on the wrong track, people will soon tell you. Because they don't want to hear you so much as what's trying to come to life through you. What you believe and what you think is very important, because it's likely to come rushing out of you when you least expect it or when you've least planned it.

Mars/Venus in New Phase
Venus is zero to forty-five degrees ahead of Mars.

What you learn to value in life is extremely important to you, because you're likely to go after it with a passion. You're not the type to think about what you love or care about; you're the type to feel it and move upon it. Many astrologers have called this a passionate position for the animal energies of the individual (which Mars and Venus are). I would rather call it spontaneous. Some call it oversexed. I'd rather call it uncontrived. You're not one to hold back when you feel something or when you want something. You should probably realize that.

You should also realize that when you're in love, you radiate a charm that draws to you what you desire–not necessarily what's best for you or what's most ennobling. Being in love is very important to you. It brings your life alive. It makes you stand out. All you have to ask is this: What am I in love with? Is it a person, an idea, a creation, or a style of life? Whatever it is, what you value (Venus) you will spontaneously seek and reach out for (Mars). You were made to plunge into life and learn as you go along–in love, in action, in creativity. This is a powerful position for radiating animal charm. Know what you're doing and use it spontaneously in that knowledge.

Saturn/Jupiter in New Phase
Jupiter is zero to forty-five degrees ahead of Saturn.

Your way to making it in the practical world is to follow what you were taught. You have an instinct for going just so far in practical things and no farther. Sometimes you will chafe at this–that something in you knows what's practical and knows just as well what's not; it doesn't always follow a well thought out pattern that you can rationalize. It comes from instinct. It comes from things you were taught that you often can't remember.

You, and a number of other people, born within about three years of one another, came into the world at the beginning of a twenty-year economic cycle. What you picked up in early life gives you an instinctive key to such cycles, though you may not be able to rationalize it very well. Whenever you want to go overboard on something, there's a danger signal that rings inside. Whenever you're becoming too stuck in a rut, there's a force in you that will say take another step forward. You would do well to follow these instincts. They're preserving you in practical terms. You don't have to think much about them–you can follow them and devote your time to other things in you that practical instincts will almost automatically support.

You're not the type who has to carve out a new world for yourself or others. You fit in the times as they are in practical terms. This only becomes a danger when the times call for radical change. Your instincts, however, will probably tell you when that time comes. And you can become a personality in your own right because you follow such instincts.

Uranus/Saturn in New Phase
Saturn is zero to forty-five degrees ahead of Uranus.

Whether you realize it or not, you have the power to become an unconscious force for leadership in your own generation. Your urge to be more than what society has taught will galvanize you into action–particularly in early life.

It is people like yourself, a number of you born during a six-year period, who always set up the major social changes for generations. Every forty-five years there is a group like you and they tend to revolt against the past–against what's dead, what's dying, and what's become obsolete. It isn't contrived; it isn't even planned. It erupts out of you and people like you. It is the urge to be something more than a social automaton. It is the urge to follow a virtually spiritual voice inside that says, "The time has come for individuals to arise again. The time has come for you to be one as others have feared to be one."

The Saturn part of this human mechanism represents individuals as they have been, and become calcified, in society. The Uranus side of it represents the voice of a generation that is beyond society's teaching patterns. It is the conscience of the generation and it calls for new individuals to meet new times. You don't have to think about it; you certainly don't have to plan it. The past and the future are battling together inside you. It is usually the future that wins and erupts out of you. If you can't listen to it as the individual your total birth chart makes you, then you will certainly see it emerging in the others around you.

Psychologically, this combination of planets represents the individuation process as it acts through groups, or generations, of individuals. This position of the Uranus/Saturn combination, after their conjunction every forty-five years, represents the spontaneous beginning of a new cycle of individuation. It erupts through people born at the beginning of the cycle. They represent its style, and often its content, without thinking about it, without even trying to do it. They set the tone for forty-five years of individuals who will follow them. In the twentieth century, this position is contained in the birth charts of those born in the late 1890s, early 1940s, and the late 1980s.

Its overall meaning is represented by the degree of the zodiac at which the two planets meet every forty-five years. It is carried out, in eight phases of the forty-five year cycle. But those who come at the beginning live it out impulsively, spontaneously, unconsciously. They are the leaders, the performers, the stylists, and the instigators of what will move in a wave and be realized or defeated at the opposition of the two planets about twenty-three years after they meet and set this process of individuation in motion across a generation.

Worker

Crescent Moon:

Moon is forty-five to ninety degrees ahead of Sun.

Getting yourself out of the pattern of traditions that surrounded you at birth is the one overriding and essential goal of your life. This could mean you were born into a family whose financial, intellectual, emotional, or spiritual orientations do not fit what is instinctively coming to life in you as an individual in your own right.

Your life is likely to be slow in unfolding. Some would even call it plodding. But this is because you are a good worker and a dependable person. You were taught to be. But you were also taught something else that is not really you. That something else is that you must carry on under the same conditions as the past. This is not true. And the more you listen to it, the more you will become engaged in a great struggle within yourself. Sometimes this struggle seems to be just below the level of consciousness – you feel it, rather than understand it. Other times it will surface in vivid symbols that strike you as being vital and emotional in nature.

These symbols, which come before you not because you chose them but because they seem to haunt you, are essentially correct in what they're trying to show you – that the past is all around you, but you are emerging out of it and you are the future. You represent the new engaged in struggle with the past which wants to hold on and shape you in its own dying image. The old – sometimes your family, sometimes the tradition in which you were born, sometimes just what is expected of you – hangs on in what seems like a death grip. And you must break it. You mustn't let it cling to you, shape you, or direct you. You *do* represent a new development. You're the future of a past form which is obsolete. You must adopt a new psychological form for a new time, though the spirit of the past may live on through you – in a different shape, in a different time.

The spirit of the past, and not its ghosts, should live through you.

This may require a complete break with family, early surroundings, or your society–directed development – whatever may have been planned for you. Too much that is antiquated is trying to hang on and draw life through you. Many people born under your personality type let the past cling to them and they simply die in life because what is dead sucks life from them. Your life won't be really easy. It will require stubborn and persistent work. And it is being shaped in you every day in what you do and what you become–and that is not likely to be what was planned for you, dreamed for you, or hoped for you by predecessors who might like to live vicariously through you. Their goals, in the abstract, may, but their particulars may not unless you give up. You carry a burden, but it is the burden of an actual beginning of something new that is taking shape out of what is dying to give what is eternal in every form a chance to live in a new time and new mold.

51°

Moon is within orb of a fifty-one degree, twenty-six minute aspect with the Sun, while ahead of it.

The above described personality is you, but doubly so. You will probably feel that fate has inexplicably interceded in your life on a number of occasions to make you feel your destiny with a poignancy. You will probably feel that you must break from the past or face a worthless living death.

Shattering breaks with the past and tradition will probably enter your life. Seemingly fate-directed events, which can shock or reorient you, may mark the pattern of your whole life. They are all aimed at one purpose: to make you realize that many (not just you or your own life) depend on your ability to become something new and to leave an inspiration through the act of doing so. Courage may be required of you; faith and sacrifice often demanded. No matter what it requires, you must bring the new to life through yourself or life will be worthless and the process stopped right here, right now, in what you fail to do.

60°

The Moon is within orb of a sixty degree aspect with the Sun, but ahead of it.

It will probably not be as difficult for you, as for others born under the Crescent Moon, to move forward on the decision to make your breaks with the past. It will become a process that is probably second nature once you set it in motion. You will see how it can be done effectively and all you will have to do is decide to move with the urges within you. You can be tremendously successful in denying the forms of the past yet carrying on their spirit in what you do. Once you set your mind to it, your methods match your aims, very easily. You are also productive in what you do when you get going and you may even receive the cooperation of the tradition in building its future forms into life.

Saturn/Moon in the Crescent Phase
Moon is forty-five to ninety degrees ahead of Saturn.

Your great struggle in life will be to adopt an identity that will take you out of the past and put you on the road to the future. This will undoubtedly be a struggle because your aims, and the methods you've been taught, are often antagonistic to one another. What you must remember is that you have to learn to be flexible in adapting your methods to what you want to be and do. The past will not tell you how to do this. In fact, the past will often make impossible your real goals until you realize you have been taught antiquated methods, habits, and responses to life. When you realize it, though, you will also recognize that it may take a new name, a new face, and surely a new attitude, to become more flexible to life.

If these two planets are in orb of the forty-five degree aspect, you may struggle hard for a new identity but life will mobilize you to it or make you feel that continuing along the old liens is futile and frustrating.

If they're within orb of sixty degrees, you will find it easier to change your patterns; all it will require is a decision and consistent effort.

If they are within the seventy-two degree orb, your own creative abilities will make the change easy and effective once you decide to listen to them and follow them through. Whatever the aspect is, follow the feeling that you need a new portrayal of yourself–something that didn't come entirely from parents, tradition, or teaching–to realize yourself as you can be.

Jupiter/Mercury in the Crescent Phase
Mercury is forty-five to ninety degrees ahead of Jupiter.

You are the individual who will find it a struggle to communicate what you really think and what you really want because you've probably been so trained in expressing yourself within a dying, or at least obsolete, tradition of making your way in society.

It will be important that when you want to get your ideas across, you do not cling to what has proved successful for others. You may not be adept or facile in getting yourself across, but if you follow your inner feelings in attempting to do so, what you are trying to say and do will gradually emerge from your actions and your being. In other words, you are the individual who finds it difficult to get yourself across as you'd like to; who even finds it difficult, at times, to get along in society as you'd like to. Don't let this bother you. Just realize a simple thing: you are feeling your way through. It will take time. You won't always be articulate. But you must persist and you must realize that what's been done by others isn't going to work for you the way it did for them. Follow your inner urges; let them lead the way even if you can't clearly see it. Yes, even stumble if you must. The integrity of what you're trying to become and do is much more important than the surface appearance.

The struggle will be pronounced at the forty-five degree aspect (it will mobilize your life and energy); it is easier at the sixty degree aspect when you find a new method you can put your energies into, and probably very easy at the seventy-two degree aspect once you find a way that is uniquely your own and that doesn't belong to someone else.

Mars/Venus in the Crescent Phase

Venus is forty-five to ninety degrees ahead of Mars.

If anything in your life is going to be noticeable, it will be the agonies and struggles you go through to realize what it is you want through love and through creative activity. This struggle will diminish, in love, when you realize that the classic ideas you've been taught about it are really just so much illusion. They don't have much to do with what you are or are trying to become through loving another.

You can expect great troubles with that facet of your life until you realize that the person you are looking for is the one who is going to encourage you to leave the past behind and not try to live in it or imitate it. This may take you a long time to realize and the agony of it may separate you from family, friends, tradition, and anything that was expected of you. But if your love life is an embarrassment, it is for this reason: You were meant to live in and for the future and love is part of that living–the shame is not in you but in what you tried to be or live out that was not the you that was coming to life.

If you are a creative person, engaged in a life of expressing yourself through art, your struggles will be poignant and yet powerful. You may try to hang around the classical forms and the classical methods, but none of them will really work for you until you put the sweat and reality of your own existence into them and reshape them into what is struggling through you for existence in its own right and form and not that of the past. Let the agony remold the past. That's what it's for.

If the aspect is near forty-five degrees, the struggle will be powerful (you may need several big blows from life to realize that classical form is not really you); near sixty degrees, there will probably be less pain and you only have to make the decision to follow your real feelings; near seventy-two degrees, you have self-expressive creative power (individualistic and past-denying) to put into anything you love or anything you attempt to do.

Saturn/Jupiter in the Crescent Phase
Jupiter is forty-five to ninety degrees ahead of Saturn.

Your life will probably be marked by the struggle to realize what reality is becoming in your own time. The old ideas about money, how to make a living, and being practical are probably what you are going to have to abandon. They can be so drilled into you, though, that it may require failure in practical terms to get you to realize that you can feel your way through economically once you have a reason of your own to do so.

You can use old methods but you can't let them use you. You can build and reshape the past and you should. An inner voice will tell you how. It may take time and patience, and you'll never be the flash success, but you can get through with your own integrity of being. And yesterday's solutions are not yours, though the eternal integrity of building through effort is.

If the aspect is near forty-five degrees, the circumstances of life will mobilize you into realizing this, probably through one or two painful economic failures. You must build patiently and slowly and your real method is what you learn as you go along. If it's near sixty degrees, you will probably learn fast. A decision to follow inner impulses is what will make you productive and economically dependable. If it's near seventy-two degrees, you'll probably come up with a unique method of your own for handling the realities of life; if you do, don't ever listen to other voices outside – they'll only ruin what you've patiently built.

Uranus/Saturn in the Crescent Phase
Saturn is forty-five to ninety degrees ahead of Uranus.

Your process of individuation is one of leaving the past behind because you realize the future is going to live only if you and others of your generation refuse to let the ghosts of the past cling to you, teach you, mold you, and live through you.

Your generation is the one that follows the impulse of those born about six years before who spontaneously uttered the vision. But you have to do more. You have to struggle through life to make it live. This may require shattering breaks with parents, society, and formal education. The integrity of what the future means can live slowly through you because you decided to make the effort that it requires to be real, to be more than a slogan.

Activist
Fighter, Pusher, Doer

First Quarter Moon:
Moon is ninety to 135 degrees ahead of the Sun.

Action, whether of the mind or of the body, is the keynote of your life. You plunge in where others often hesitate. You act to rid yourself, or the atmosphere in which you're operating, of what you consider to be obsolete and outworn. You know it has to go in order that what is trying to be can have clear ground upon which to grow. This urge in you, to tear down the relics of the past, is an instinct. It moves you, motivates you, often goads you. Where others will talk, and still others will move patiently and slowly, you have the urge to act. Because of this, you live in a stimulating world–one that is filled with the sound of challenging words or challenging activities.

You, too, can move people, but sometimes to fury because you are ready to cancel the past now without being clear in your mind or your words what's going to replace it. You don't worry about that because you know that what frustrates people's self-expression is an obstacle and must be gotten out of the way. If there is anyone capable of plunging into a dying situation and managing it into new life, the true concept of which can hardly be seen until it emerges out of what is developing naturally through itself, it is you. You're the person they were talking about in this saying: "He plunges in where angels fear to tread."

This is because you have a vision–or let's say the feeling of a vision. It's never very clear in your mind and you have trouble articulating it lucidly, but finally it emerges out of your action and your energy. It makes you a manager, eventually, but one who learns to manage through activity and not through a thought out plan.

You're likely to have a number of fights in your life–physical or verbal. And these fights are really with the remnants of the past. You can't tolerate them; you have to irritate them or get them out of your way. Whether you realize it or not, you're a social force to be reckoned with. You believe in the right of people to express themselves and you won't be constrained by tradition.

You may work quietly, depending on your total disposition, but you're sure to work energetically. It could be a situation, a way of life, a manner of expressing the true person–it doesn't matter what it is; what's important is that you will act out what is trying to come to life through you and others. And you'll do it without real fear because you believe that the future, though unclear in total concept and detail, is an irresistible force that you're ready to follow and through it, find your shape. And that's what you have to do–plunge in, clear away the structures of the past that are outmoded, and move energetically toward that which you have faith is good for others as well as yourself.

120°

Moon is in orb of a 120 degree aspect with the Sun while being ahead of it.

You, too, are an activist, but one who moves easily through the surroundings that might prove frustrating to others of your kind. You may not make as much noise–it would seem to those watching–but you accomplish as much as one who does. This is because you have a kind of style that matches your inner goals without being jarring in any way.

There is a kind of security you exude to others–that they can trust you even if you're shattering some of their cherished props right in front of their eyes. This is because you seem to have a kind of anchor attached to you that makes it seem, sometimes, like you're standing still when you're really not. In other words, your manners and gestures often belie your real goals and people go along with, them, not because they understand what's going on inside you but because they trust you. You have a tremendous ability to effect change without making waves. This should not lull you into a sleep–for it could–but should move you even more to make the changes you know will benefit people.

Saturn/Moon First Quarter
Moon is ninety degrees to 135 degrees ahead of Saturn.

You can be an aggressive person in putting yourself forward and letting people know who you think you are. In the early part of your life,
this was probably because you were taught to fight for your name. In the second part of your life, it can be because you are living out, through your own identity, a conflict that was more in your parents than in you–though you picked up a lot of it and are trying to throw it off. The only way to do this is to make enough noise that it gets outside you.

When you find your own real identity, it will probably be another aggressive one. You will realize that you are a person who has to create a name for yourself, breaking from the bonds of the past and establishing yourself in a framework that's free of them. This may involve a lot of talk and speaking out. It could also involve some sharp confrontations with people around you or people who tried to shape you in their image.

When you feel you've got to be someone else, though you don't really know who, you're on the right track. Go ahead and do it. It will never be entirely clear to you just what identity you are establishing, but that's not as important as doing it. It will become clearer and clearer what it is with each false concept of the past that you throw off your new self.

Jupiter/Mercury First Quarter
Mercury is ninety to 135 degrees ahead of Jupiter.

You are the communicator who can move people to action. You're also the person who can jar others with what you think, what you say, and the way you go about taking care of yourself in any situation. You have an aggressive survival instinct, one that tells you there are some ideas and some ways of communicating that are simply dead and it's time to plunge into the situation and let some new ones emerge.

We could say you're a fighty talker, an aggressive thinker, a com¬bative communicator. You don't want the past in your way when you think or talk and you look to the future with a kind of faith, though the ideas it represents may not be terribly clear. Still, you know they're worth acting for, whatever they may become. You have faith in little more than their dim outlines. But it is out of just such dim premonitions that the figure always arises.

If the aspect of Jupiter and Mercury is near ninety degrees, you're the type who often goes overboard in what you say, who will stretch an idea as far as it will go–and sometimes farther.

If the aspect is near 120 degrees, you'll still have the combative ring to what you do, but it will come off to people as being easy to listen to. Words and ideas could flow through you easily without your always realizing their impact or portent. But, speak up, say what you feel–it's leading to change and you know that change, not stagnancy, is the true state of living matter.

Mars/Venus First Quarter

Venus is ninety to 135 degrees ahead of Mars.

Your love life, the emotional tenor of your being, and your approach to creative activity is one of "do it now and analyze it later." You're an activist in what you feel, with the people you love and in all you do that you enjoy or feel is an expression of yourself. This means you'll probably run after what you care for and let the chips fall where they may, that your relationships with people can be a kind of a storm on wheels and that pleasure, for you, is doing, being, acting on the moment.

Why do you live like this? Because you know that the "proper" way of doing things is only an excuse for doing and being nothing–or for avoiding what only the daring would seek or become. The old ideas about love, about art, about what one values and what he seeks, are a kind of living frustration to you and your self-expression. You must clear them from your life and seek what you know lies just beyond them if only someone would commit himself to being now, at this moment, and in these actions which can entirely contradict what has gone before through other people.

Some may say you live in misery and others may worry that you're too much of an aggressor–in their words you burn the candle at both ends. You might as well laugh now because it may be necessary later.

Your energies were made for action, not contemplation, and you learn as you experience. Your love life, and your creative endeavors, probably do resemble a storm. But they produce and you live through them. That's more than many can say.

If the Mars/Venus aspect is near 120 degrees, you're probably the type who can easily attract what you seek in people and in activity. In fact, you may indulge yourself in both without feeling you've known the truth of either. Yours can be a case of too much too soon–or an easy path through life built on others' feelings. If you're an artist, you'll have your own special touch that will make it easy to convey to another what you feel even if the other does not understand its true content.

Saturn/Jupiter First Quarter
Jupiter is ninety to 135 degrees ahead of Saturn.

Your struggle for survival in society's crystallized ways of making a living is probably a battle and a constant fight. One way or another you're going to cause some people a little agony as you go about the process of living in practical terms. You're the type to overcommit yourself, to ignore what others would call common sense in practical matters. Well, what are you really doing in all this (because if the aspect is near 120 degrees you'll coast through but you will probably overindulge yourself in practical things)?

You probably don't realize it, but you're paving the way–through instinct, intuition and taking a chance–for some new ways of making it in practical terms to come into being. You're the type who can walk into an old method of making a living and tear it apart or make it glut itself. Once this is done you face a crisis: What can replace what you've helped destroy?

Action, new methods, energy geared to a new motive and method, is your real solution to any such critical state of affairs. Plunge in and see if there isn't a different way that fits into a different time. Maybe you don't possess the common sense of yesterday, but your very actions can manage a new kind of common sense into being. This may not be recognized during your own time but it will probably be honored by some who follow. And the reason is simple. You took an old situation that was dying in its own rigidity and carved a new way of living into being.

If the aspect is near 120 degrees, the common sense of the past is probably easy for you to manipulate, but boring at the same time. You could coast along and die in the old methods; you could also decide there is a creative new way to do things and readily get people to go along with you, even if you don't' clearly see the new method until it's emerging from what you're doing as you do it.

Uranus/Saturn First Quarter
Saturn is ninety to 135 degrees ahead of Uranus.

You're the activist, the street fighter, the aggressor, the warrior of your generation trying to find and express its own individuality. You're the group of people who will stand and shout, "Clear away the past; destroy the establishment–we mean it!" You aren't content to work in the old system because you know that part of its very structure is what is keeping you from expressing yourself. You feel it must be plowed out of the way before you'll be able to go on and be what is demanding to come to life inside you.

You're not very articulate at expressing what this new thing is, but you are vehement and frighteningly visionary in determining what, out of the past, is the real obstacle in the way of the future. Society has reason to fear you. You'll not only take to the street and demonstrate for what you want; you'll physically and verbally destroy what's standing in your way in the process.

If the aspect is near 120 degrees, you may even get more cooperation than you expect. Whatever happens, you're the surge into action, into the streets, and into battle for your generation's urge to be.

Analyst

Gibbous Moon:
Moon is 135 to 180 degrees ahead of the Sun.

You're conscientious, analytical, and full of questions–a lot of them about where you fit into the scheme of things and how you can make your best contribution to living and to society. Sometimes you're a kind of perfectionist and it always helps you find a method that will allow you to fit into things without wasting effort.

You may have to spend a number of periods of apprenticeship discovering what is the method that can make you a better functioning human being. That phrase–better functioning–is important. You're the type who will look at those who have preceded you in life or in any particular endeavor and decide that they've wasted a lot of energy considering what has been accomplished. You would like to find a better method, a better way–one that allows less waste and still accomplishes.

Because of this, you are the type to question everything around you. Why is it done that way? What's the reason? What does it all accomplish? You have an instinctive need to find the answers to these questions and so you become quite verbal in seeking them out. You are probably the one person, in any situation, who will demand to know why?

When young, you are probably noted for this. You're the questioning type. Many people, then, will probably be irritated by it, but you will persist because the question isn't exactly conscious–it's a need that seems to move out of you.

Once you have found a method, you can become a stickler for details. You can also become a worrywart, unless you realize that each individual has different capabilities and each one requires his own method–not necessarily the one that worked for you or that worked for another, but the one that will work, uniquely, for him. You should understand this because, after all, that's what you demanded of life yourself. You're the type who learns thoroughly and needs to find his own method and, because of that, it is good for you to spend time in periods of apprenticeship–whether they are physical, mental, emotional, or spiritual in nature. There is a way for everyone who seeks not to waste or not to be spiritually useless and you're the type who will find it and help others find their own as well.

144°

Moon is within orb of a 144 degree aspect of the Sun but still ahead of it.

You're not only an analyst but an efficiency expert when you put your mind to it. In fact, once you've found the way, your ability to produce through it is almost phenomenal. You're the type who can learn how to be productive by applying a certain type of technique. And often you don't really have to seek it out; you just have to find out what it applies to, because it is an integral part of you. Where others are creative in concept, you are creative in technique and you were born with a capacity to apply it so well that the irritations others feel from people born under the Gibbous Moon will probably not be aimed at you. You not only can question, but demonstrate that you had good reason to do so.

150°

Moon is within orb of a 150 degree aspect of the Sun but still ahead of it.

You are the analyst and perfectionist who is most likely to become hung up in his methods and techniques and forget what they are for. You can become so absorbed in the system you have learned that it becomes difficult for you to adapt to changing conditions around you. This is because your habits, which have become rigidly conditioned to method in many cases, have overwhelmed your original aims. This will not only frustrate you, but irritate others to the point where they may feel you're goading them into action against you. You must learn flexibility and adaptation and never forget that methods are the tools of goals and not the other way around. Methodology is your forte; but it can become your prison.

Saturn/Moon Gibbous

Moon is 135 to 180 degrees ahead of Saturn.

Your parents or your society may have so conditioned you when you were young that it will be necessary to spend a period of analysis, between the ages of twenty-one and thirty, to discover just who you are and where you fit into the scheme of things that is actually evolving around you, rather than what parents or society hoped would evolve around you.

This position often indicates a subtle hostility or alienation between the parents that affects the child–in this case, you. They could have been goads to one another and you caught between them. They could have been so caught up in what they were doing to be materially productive that they tried to make you a machine. Or they could have simply irritated one another and set your psyche up for a reevaluation once you got out on your own. You'll have to question your early teachings and see what a waste some of them have been. Your apprenticeship will be to learn what it is you can identify with what will make you productive or worthwhile as a person.

If the aspect between the two is 135 degrees, the urge to find a new identity will be a mobilizing force in your life. If it is near 144 degrees, there will probably be special techniques you can learn for adapting yourself better to the world as you will live in it. If it's near 150 degrees, you could become all hung up in identity that pits you against your better self and have to spend some time learning how your idea of yourself is in conflict with habits you've picked up that don't fit it.

Jupiter/Mercury Gibbous
Mercury is 135 to 180 degrees ahead of Jupiter.

You are the type of communicator and operator who can work better with a method for speaking or presenting yourself than you can function spontaneously. There's a spontaneous side to you–you love asking questions that occur on the moment. And you're a kind of analyst when you really get going.

But this is an irritating thing to many of the people around you and you will probably find that eventually you will come across better when you think of the technique you are using in communicating with people. You will find at least one that will work every time and will seem to be a kind of energy saver for you. I'm not saying you're contrived (though you could be if you got so hung up in a style or technique that you never tried anything else, especially on people of different natures), but I'm saying that you learn, often through experiences that waste your time, that you should prepare what you're going to say or think it out in advance.

If the aspect is near 135 degrees, you can be a brilliant, even provocative, analyst in your thinking, speaking, or writing. If it's near 144 degrees, your personal techniques in communication will probably become a hallmark of your life. If it's near 150 degrees you will have a tendency to stick with one technique slavishly to your own detriment; it will often be necessary to look anew at situations and adopt unexpected courses of action and communication to find your way out of a rut.

Mars/Venus Gibbous
Venus is 135 to 180 degrees ahead of Mars.

You're the type of person who is likely to analyze your motives and desires to the point of others' distraction, and yet enjoy doing these very things. What you find yourself reaching out for in love is often not what you'd want once you get it. Your motive in creative expression often doesn't match your vision or even your style.

I wonder if you'd believe that you may have to spend a period of apprenticeship learning how to love or how to create in the manner that best expresses you, rather than what might be fun because it's sensational. Whether you believe it or not, you're likely to find this true at some point in your life. In other words, a lot of your efforts in love and creativity are a waste until you do analyze what you're doing and whether it fits what you really want and value.

If the aspect is near 135 degrees, analysis of this aspect of you will be made imperative by life; near 144 degrees, it can be solved easily by personal techniques you possess but may not have brought into action; near 150 degrees, you'll tend to bog down in others' ways and methods and be forced to find your own sometimes out of desperation.

Saturn/Jupiter Gibbous
Jupiter is 135 to 180 degrees ahead of Saturn.

In order to function practically in this world, you're going to have to analyze what you're doing. You need a method very badly because your concepts of conservatism and openhandedness are in irritating conflict with one another. It is best for you to learn a working method for handling practical problems, one from which you do not deviate very far. You're also the type who learns best in actual apprenticeship rather than from formal learning. This will probably be critical to a job or career for you. Eventually you'll learn to handle waste and ineffi¬ciency–two things that can mark your life until you analyze its practical dimensions.

Near 135 degrees, this can be acute. Around 144 degrees, it can be solved through learning productive techniques at which you're talented. Near 150 degrees, you're probably hung up in obsolete methods and need to learn new ones for new situations.

Uranus/Saturn Gibbous
Saturn is 135 to 180 degrees ahead of Uranus.

Your group is the evaluating side of a generation that came to life about sixteen years before you were born. You can see its wastes, its excesses, and its failures. You've watched the instigators, the strugglers, and the activists. Now it's incumbent upon people like yourself to find the method that actually works in finding one's individuality.

You may look to gurus or methods of unfolding individuality. You may decide there is a method for working within the system. Whatever you decide you're likely to be less noisy than your predecessors–though you will ask embarrassing and acute questions of the established order– and you're likely to decide they wasted effort that you don't want to waste. You sift, you analyze and then you decide: "There is a way for me to individualize myself and I will find it and work at it."

Seeker

Full Moon:

Moon is 180 to 135 degrees behind Sun after the opposition has been made.

Of all the personality types, yours may be considered the most unstable or the most illuminated. And you must choose which it will be. There is tremendous power in you to follow the instincts of the life force that pulses through you, but there is just as much power in you to shape it to your own goals or the goals of something that is outside your animal nature (if you want to call it that).

Your life is likely to be founded or crashed upon relationships. You have the choice of seeking out what you lack in another because you feel inferior or you can seek it out because you feel full in yourself yet aware that you need a complement to it. This will be the greatest problem, or the greatest realization of your life. Yet there is one other that can surmount either. And that is the understanding that what you may lack, or are not, in the conscious side of yourself is present in the unconscious (or spiritual, if you prefer) side of yourself. You are the sum of all that mankind has evolved to, yet you are something more. You possess the ability to incorporate into it what mankind has yet feared to touch. And that is what he cannot prove through his senses.

Because of this latter aspect of your personality potential, I call you the searcher. There is good reason for this. The first is that most people born under the Full Moon listen to the animal drives of society that are instilled in them and go off in search of a great love in the form of another person. Society teaches us, in these days, that we lack in subtle ways. And so your search may be to find what you lack. Yet society also instills in us a kind of inferiority so that when we find what we lack we still hate ourselves and cannot really love it as it should be loved–not for us to possess it, but for us to give to it what it does not have in itself but which is in us.

If you are born under the Full Moon you must surely understand what it is I am saying because you have already encountered some of the inanities of the industrial, material society. It does not respect meaning and meaning is the essence of your life. It is what a person means, not what he is in quantity or form, that moves you most. Yet people totally immersed in the being of quantity do not understand you. This is why conventional relationships fail you. In despair, you may turn to God or to some great idea. But is that idea you or is it an avoidance of you? I think you must ask that question, for if you could see it–that is objectively–you would be able to realize that all you are seeking is inside yourself, on the other side of ego, on the other side of self-satisfaction, and it is the greatest compliment you could find.

Your life probably will be a search but if you could understand that one thing, it would not have to be half so unstable as it's likely to look on the record. You must abandon the record in other people's terms of valuing it. What you do does not count. What your life means does. You could do everything, or anything, from the sublime to the ridiculous and it would not matter what it looked like, or what others thought of it, as long as you found meaning or fulfillment, rather than self-justification, through it.

Bring all of yourself to life. Bring the conscious being to life in the animal body. They are not enemies. They are companions, but it is the consciousness (that we are spiritual beings) that must direct, or shape: the body, mind, and emotions, as well as the intellect (which is different from the mind). And that is what you are living out, no matter what anyone in this world may tell you. When you find the other side of yourself (whether you imagine it inside or outside you–and that's a matter of spiritual semantics, depending on what "you" is meant to be), it is what you're seeking. And there your quest of instinct ends and your incorporation of consciousness begins.

Your life isn't going to be easy, but it could be the most meaningful of all the personality types, because the conscious way is the next step in humane evolution. And you're its living example.

150°

Moon is within orb of 150 degree aspect of Sun but still behind it. If the foregoing doesn't make sense to you it's becuase you've let yourself be caught up in romantic ideals of the past. They are not what is going to lead the way into tomorrow or even exist today. The habits and attitudes your predecessors may have instilled in you are highly destructive to your real goals and being in life. You have not only to find meaning, or realize that consciousness comes before instinct, but you have got to do something about this in life. It's not a dream. It's a reality you can bring into being through becoming it.

You have a tendency to revert to the past, even to past lives, in order to escape the present. This could extend to following some great idea or some great personage without really living out what it or he says. It's easy to quote, or talk, or elaborate–but is it so easy to "be" without saying, but becoming? This is your real test. Life is now and you can be it. You can be consciousness in action. Saying what you'd like to do, rather than doing what you'd like to speak for itself, is the method of the past for ignorant and fearful men who can't see. You should realize that; only the ruts you've stuck yourself in are what are making you feel frustration with life.

144°

Moon is within orb of a 144 degree aspect with the Sun but still behind it. When all is said and done, it will be what you've done, and accomplished through it that will leave your mark on this world. Your techniques will shine through that work. Your ability to live out an idea, or bring to life in action something that is greater than the action itself is one of the great contributions you hold within yourself. You must only realize what you are doing and become involved in it; you have the style and the technique inside you. Once you find a meaningful task for it, that style will work. And what you do can be productive, not in material terms, but in spiritual meaning. Yours is the consciousness that speaks, writes, acts, or is with proficiency and specific graces.

Saturn/Moon Full
Moon is 180 to 135 degrees behind Saturn.

When it comes to identity, yours can be one of the most unstable there is in modern society. You're probably going to have to remake yourself, because it's likely that your parents were in basic conflict and you stood in the middle of them, not knowing which way to be pulled. This may not have been obvious, but it probably has had its effect on you. If it isn't parents, it's tradition and adaptability to the moment that are in conflict. Again, you are pulled between them.

You are going to have to decide, consciously, who you are and why you are and then make the decision to be a little of both of the antagonists in your life but something more as well. I could say it's your karma that you had the parents you did, or the social upbringing you experienced. Instead, I'll say you needed to see two sides of life in order to rise above the limits to either one and make something greater of yourself. Identity can be your one great problem until you realize that you can rename, or remake, yourself and do it by choice. Until you do, there will always be the pull of one side against the other, not only in forces outside you, but in imitation in what you're displaying to others through yourself.

Jupiter/Mercury Full
Mercury is 180 to 135 degrees behind Jupiter.

You're the type of person who has to think before you speak or you will find yourself in some rather jarring situations. You have an instinct to overstate yourself, to plunge into hazy ideas and make them even more confusing through your own interpretation, which you really don't think out. Some people will say you have an uncanny ability to put your foot in your mouth. Others will say you stretch things to the point of collapse and ignore common sense.

Well, it doesn't matter what they say, except that learning through others' reactions is one of the things you're doing even when it looks like it's all going against you. If you want to come across well, though, you should not speak, write, act or push yourself forward on the moment. You should think before you do any of these things. This will be critical at some points in your life, as you probably already know.

One of your problems in early life may have been the morality you were taught and the formal learning you received. They may have been in conflict with one another and your communications are the result. You should probably think that over. What shapes what you say and how do the two really coexist? You should wonder about that sometimes and you should decide what you really want to convey before you plunge into anything. Your success or failure does not rely on spontaneous wit but on considered thinking.

Mars/Venus Full
Venus is 180 to 135 degrees behind Mars.

Your love life can be sheer agony until you realize that what you go after is often in complete disharmony with what you'd like to have. Before you pursue someone, or plunge into some pleasurable activity, you ought to think about what you are doing and why you're doing it. This will relieve a lot of the frustration you experience through love and fun.

Sometimes it's a shock to another individual that your charming manner has absolutely nothing to do with what you're really wanting from him. You also have a tendency to plunge into situations without realizing where they are really leading. And if the truth were to be known, you often misrepresent yourself. This is because you have never stopped and really thought about whether your desires are anywhere in alignment with your true values.

In other words, ask yourself this question: "Is what excites me and moves my passions what I really want? Is it what I am capable of being gentle or considerate with?" When you answer that question, you'll have found one-half of the source of your personal agonies. The other half is that you need experience in order to find out what you do want and some agony is a prerequisite of it.

If you are an artist or engaged in any kind of creative activity, this position can actually be a tremendous source of power in the modern world. It is the authenticity of experience that they are afraid to have that people often seek through modern forms of art. You are in a position to speak of it, to have known it, to have achieved realization or illumination through it. If you have learned, your medium can come to life for you because you can place in it what it does not possess of itself. This is because in the agonies of love you have discovered something of the dimension of the other side of your ego-self and you have discovered, through your art form, a way of bringing it into the world that is not completely personal yet speaks profoundly of the human state.

If the aspect is near 150 degrees, you must be wary of getting into ruts in your love life and expressing yourself creatively. You must become more adaptable. If it's near 144 degrees, you'll find a technique in love, and it will get results, but you'll sometimes wonder if results are what you really wanted. If this is applied creatively, it indicates that you have techniques to apply to your art that are a personal distinction in all you do. You can be a productive individual and one who styles his work with his own life force.

Saturn/Jupiter Full
Jupiter is 180 to 135 degrees behind Saturn.

Your ability to make it in the world, in practical terms, is going to be tested, if not defeated. You should always think before you spend. You should never act on what you see others doing. Because it works for them, it doesn't mean it's going to work for you. People will say you have no common sense about money. I suspect this is true. But what will you do about it?

If you want to be successful in society's terms you are going to have to analyze a basic conflict in yourself. One side of this conflict tells you to plunge in. The other side tells you to hold back. You are caught in the middle, as well you should be. Why? Because you have to find a meaning for your practical existence and until you do it will be in severe trouble. Practicality doesn't really mean anything to you (unless it was drilled into you religiously or paternally and then you may hate it) unless it has some goal that is beyond simple production or material well being. If your life is full of social and material setbacks, it is for one reason only: Society and things have absolutely no place in your life unless they are shaped by some goal or meaning that is beyond their appear¬ances.

You will succeed when you have thought out what it is necessary to do in practical terms in order to continue what you want to do that is of meaning to your own individual existence, rather than what's convenient to fit you into a proper niche in someone else's scheme of things.

Uranus/Saturn Full
Saturn is 180 to 135 degrees behind Uranus.

In you, and others like you, will live or die the meaning of a generation's urge to be different from the ones that preceded it. You will come to a great awareness of what it really means that individuals born twenty-two years before you revolted against the established order of conventionality around them. You will also experience a great inner realization no matter what you do about it.

There is a tremendous difference between the social being and the individual being, between the established and material order, and the order of spirit that is trying to live through them. And you may be caught between both realms. What you must realize is that you can fuse them both in yourself and create in life what is neither of them, but life to them both.

You can be an individual, who is more than what society would teach you to be for convenience, because you choose to be one. You can listen to the voice of man inside yourself and decide that you will bring it to the surface in the meaning of your life, in the realizations of your thinking, in your actions, and in your being. You are the key to the great cycle of individuation: It will live in you consciously or fall apart and await another chance to live twenty-three years after you.

Believer

Disseminating Moon:
Moon is 135 to ninety degrees behind the Sun after opposition.

Where there's a significant idea to be learned, and finally to be conveyed to others, there you'll be found, learning, absorbing, feeling the force of it, and trying to bring it to life in yourself.

Of all the personality types, yours is the best for communicating. Many people like yourself are found in teaching, advertising, and the communications field–wherever there is a message to be gotten out to others. We could almost call you a natural broadcaster, for if you believe in an idea there is hardly anything that will stop you from trying to convince others of its worth. You make a fine publicist for any person of worth who is trying to convince people of what would be best for them.

Your one great problem is that once you believe in an idea you will not understand why others do not instantly come to it and accept it. You will probably even grow impatient with them and right there is a key to what has happened to you that perhaps shouldn't have. You are such a believer, once convinced, that you can also easily become a fanatic for a cause or a person who is trying to move other people. When the fanaticism overcomes you, you should pause for introspection and question whether the idea is worthwhile for everyone or just for you.

The one realization that is hard for you to make, when you're in the grip of an idea or a movement is that people are similar in some common aspects, but they are also different as individuals. What might have worked for you and your particular mindset and chemical system might not work exactly the same for another mindset and chemical system. You could rightly be called the true believer, and sometimes a great propagandist, but you could also be called intolerant at times.

You will find, during your life, that living is not worthwhile to you unless there is something you can give yourself up to. But you ought to test it, and consider it thoroughly before you plunge in so deeply that you can't get out. Some of the ideas you give yourself to could be out of desperation rather than honesty. For that's another aspect of you. The personality types have reached their apex when they reach your state of being. And without something beyond themselves to live for, almost any personality type is rather useless when one examines what life is really about.

You are superb at acting, being, demonstrating, and conveying an idea of importance–one that will benefit not only yourself but others as well. And that latter should always be kept in mind. Yes, you do need something to live for besides self-satisfaction but try not to take it out of desperation. Try to take it only after long and serious consideration. Because of all those who can evaluate an idea, a person, or an activity in honesty, and measure its true worth, you are best equipped for the task. Yet you are also so full of a need to be doing something of worth that desperation can lead you into something to do even if it's not really worth doing. You have to have some idea to love and live for. But for heaven's sake–no, for your sake and for the sake of others who will be impressed by you–know consciously the worth of what you follow. For you will surely impress people with it, one way or another.

120 degrees: Moon is within orb of the 120 degree aspect and behind the Sun. I guess I could call you the smooth talker, the smooth lover, the character who comes to many things with ease and can leave them just as easily. In fact, life could get to be quite a bore for you just because things do come to you so easily. You are the type who is most likely to coast through life, living out what society considers an ideal existence, and then discover abruptly that everything around you, and even in you, is hollow.

The trine aspect is considered good and desirable by ordinary astrology, but you can be the living proof that there is a subtle hell in much ease and too little challenge. You are the type, also, who is likely at some point in his life to find that he has been duped by an idea or a person, because it was so easy to go along with either. You'd better question what's too easy because someday you will be rudely awakened to its real worth. You can drift through life if you wish, but you'll find life is more vivid and certainly more meaningful when you are doing something that affects others' lives so that they become more deep and meaningful.

Saturn/Moon Disseminating

Moon is 135 to ninety degrees behind Saturn.

Whether you like them or not, because of their individual quirks compared to yours, your parents probably fulfilled the role you needed from an authority figure and a teacher in your life. If the aspect here is around 135 degrees, this is not so true as if it's closer to 120 degrees. Nevertheless, you were probably taught to convey yourself well to others.

There should be no doubt, in early life, about who you are or what you're really doing. But in the second part of life, just because the first was so easy in that way, you're the one who might experience a profound identity crisis because you're going to have to change who you are and what you are doing. You're a natural communicator of yourself and what was taught you. In fact, sometimes you will probably be puzzled because others are not like you at all. But it might not bother you. You could simply consider that they are not what they should be, as you see it.

This will all be fine until you really go on your own. Then you will realize that what you're conveying to others about yourself is no longer supported by the past and you need to know its source and its reason for being in order that it will work for you. You will also be the kind of personality who can challenge your surroundings to give you an identity–one that's worth living and worth being. You have to find an idea of yourself and then put substance into it. Once you do, you not only talk it, but live it out. And that's what will impress others.

Jupiter/Mercury Disseminating
Mercury is 135 to ninety degrees behind Jupiter.

Your morality and your ideas are things you should examine closely because you will be a living portrayal of them. They undoubtedly will not remain hidden. You are the communicator extraordinaire. You not only can take an idea and convey it vividly, but you can know precisely how you did it and why you did it. You, consciously, can be the best writer, teacher, communicator in your group of peers.

You will want to have something to use this talent for. And that's what I mean about your ideas and your morality. If you don't find something outside yourself, you will undoubtedly convey, with conviction, what you were taught to believe when you were young. We all go through changes, however, and even life and its goals change. In the modern world, moralities and ideas change rapidly. And this could set you back because you could go on passionately clinging to and broadcasting a philosophy that is simply outdated to the situations that are most demanding.

If the aspect is near 135 degrees, you can be a provocative and challenging communicator and easily stir up your surroundings to what they need to face. If it's near 120 degrees, you'll have an ease and grace in your talk, your gestures, and often in your very being. In fact, it could all be too easy. Whatever your situation, however, you ought to find out the motives behind what you do as well as the technique that works for you.

Mars/Venus Disseminating
Venus is 135 to ninety degrees behind Mars.

Whenever I think of the individual who wants to live a life or a love modeled on a classic example, you come to mind. I have no doubt that you can be a great romantic, but I wonder if you really love the person or the idea of loving. It will be so easy to try to duplicate what you feel is beautiful that I think you really ought to consider the possibility of following what is deeply in you, rather than what you see on the outside that has impressed you. The great loves that history and literature record were part of their times, and they frequently were not remembered as such while the participants were living.

You ought to consider that there is some real meaning, or message, you could live out through love. There is also a message incorporated in what you create. And in both cases, you ought to be consciously aware of what the real motive is behind what you are doing. For it is that motive that makes you vivid; without it or realizing it fully, you can be acting out a parody and even a dead gesture.

If the aspect is near 135 degrees, you'll challenge your surroundings through what you love and what you create. If it's near 120 degrees, it will be easy to get an idea across just by being in love, just by taking part in throes of creating in whatever form you choose. Remember, the classical examples will be easy to imitate. Is that what you want to do–just imitate? Why not create and be what is you that you would like others to see and be impressed by, even if it has no precedent?

Saturn/Jupiter Disseminating
Jupiter is 135 to ninety degrees behind Saturn after the opposition.

You were born after the turning point of a great economic cycle that affected the whole society into which you were born. It should have learned to consciously manage its economics, though it may have tried instead to escape the consequences of them. Whatever happened, it was impressed on your surroundings when you were growing up and taking in your first impressions of the world. Because of this, you may not realize it, but you have an instinct for managing in practical affairs that you can bring to the surface of your mind if you will.

You're also the type who can take an idea and make it into money or into what you need in practical dimensions. You could be the person who will talk your way in and out of financial crisis and monetary ups and downs. Probably one of your greatest assets, once you realize it and put it to use, is your ability to convey an idea and make it take vivid shape in others' eyes. You can develop a kind of sixth sense about money and practicality. And you can turn it on or off at your own command.

If this aspect is near 135 degrees, you will probably be challenged to put this practical sense to use. If it's near 120 degrees, you'll often be doing it without thinking much about it–it will have become second nature. The fields of teaching, communication, writing, and public relations are naturals for you once you find the idea that you feel you can support or live out. They are often more practical ways of making a living for you than what others would call solid work. But that's because you're a professional with ideas, once you find one you can believe in. And you can convince others of their worth because you can be a living example of it in action.

Uranus/Saturn Disseminating
Saturn is 135 to ninety degrees behind Uranus after the opposition.

You are the personality mankind's unconscious dreamed of twenty-five years before it erupted with new ideas and new approaches to life. The people born six years before you had to incorporate into or reject from their lives those ideas and approaches that could make a living individual out of what could have easily become a social automaton.

Whatever they did about that, you can do more. You can take those ideas that only found fledgling shape in the people who came before you and live them out with meaning and vividness. If you don't, you'll find that your life is somehow hollow, that it's easy to get on the bandwagon of some novel idea and ride it out without realizing where it's going. You have a choice and a significant one. You can consciously decide to be an individual who is of worth not only to society, but to men in general and to the future.

You'll need an idea to follow, to live out. Choose it carefully. Test it thoroughly. For you are an example, if you find what's worth doing or being. And what you do will impress others because you mean it. You can challenge your world with your being and inform it with your beliefs.

Changer

Last Quarter Moon:
Moon is ninety to forty-five degrees behind the Sun after opposition

You're the quiet one, the competent person who carries beneath his tidy surface the slowly growing need for a tumultuous or at least dramatic change. You're the type who goes through life presenting a facade of one shape while preparing, inside, what could be its total contradiction.

There is at least one major change of direction, goal-orientation, or personality that will mark your life. This is because you are taught to be adept at what is dying or obsolete and you can only be bored, in reality, until you can do what is needed and what may be quite new. You're probably bound to shock those who knew you in one way and are not prepared to comprehend you in one that is growing definitely and even purposely, though they never seem to see it until it emerges full blown.

This is one of your reasons for being secretive. You are nurturing, inside, something that you don't trust the world with until it matures in you and then becomes you. You are the individual who must commit his life to the future rather than the past, even if you are thoroughly adept at existing in the mold and the manner of the past. You are likely to be misunderstood, too, because you will not announce what is growing in you until you feel you are ready. And then when you do, you peg it to principle and often a kind of principle that you do not articulate very well.

You could be called a mystery to many people. They just won't understand why you did what you did when you chose to do it. Some of them will weep and others will shake their heads, but once you've made the commitment, you will only become firmer in your conviction. You will refuse to live in the past and will abandon it. Many revolutionary characters have been born in your personality type. And those who have refused to change or follow the spirit inside have died, also. There seems to be a hardening, a rigidity of what is obsolete in them, that leads them into shattering situations that easily crack them. So change, at least one major life-altering change, appears to be a hallmark of your life_

And when you learn that change, at any time, is a life-renewing process and not a threat, except to what's already dying psychologically, you become an inspiration to everyone around you. They may not take to it at first, and that's why you have developed the stoic attitude that marks you, but eventually they will not be able to ignore it or put it down. All of this is conscious—you know what you are doing and when you're going to do it, though you keep it all inside until you're ready—so there is no reason to weep for you. There's only reason to encourage you. You're the type who keeps otherwise boring lives from descending to a bottomless rut.

72°

Moon is seventy-two degrees behind the Sun after opposition. You're the type who will make a life, direction, or goal change because it's the creative thing to do and it's a personal expression of all the latent abilities that hid behind what you were taught and tried to perform in the spirit of what taught you. You choose, too, but you choose what you do because it's an expression of your own individual reality rather than being an expression of what made you competent in terms outside that individuality that was brewing, slowly but surely, inside.

60°

Moon is sixty degrees behind the Sun after opposition. You're the type who will make a change by gradually altering your methods to suit your new goals. You probably won't shock others as much by your changes as will those types born nearer the ninety degree aspect of this personality type. You're also the individual who wants to be productive in all you do. You can see, by analyzing the situation consciously, what is outmoded in your life. You can also see what's unproductive. Because of this perception you possess, you can make changes without a lot of fuss. You may be just as secretive in going about them but you take them one by one and because what emerges comes out gradually, it has less immediate impact on those around you and yet goes just as far, in depth and meaning, as what might jolt them.

Saturn/Moon Last Quarter

Moon is ninety to forty-five degrees after Saturn following opposition.

A major change of identity will probably occur in your life because you choose to effect it. This could be because your parents and your society tried to shape you into something that was unfitting to your true, individual goals in life once you became aware there was an individual inside that wanted out. It could also be that your parents were in conflict with one another in a psychological way and you grew up with a need to resolve, or get out of, that conflict.

Your identity change could go so far as a change of name that would dissolve the psychological ghosts you can see clinging to you through what your early upbringing molded you into that you did not choose for yourself. In other words, a lot of what you become could be a reaction to what people tried to make you from the outside, rather than trying to bring alive what was really in you. And your very name can be a kind of magic wand that renews in you what is not appropriate to your real self. The important thing, though, is that you consciously choose the identity you would like and then go about creating it in yourself. This will often require a rooting out of responses that you were taught, that don't allow you to express your real self.

If the aspect is near seventy-two degrees, you can creatively choose a new identity, one that will allow you to express yourself, almost artistically, as the individual you imagine you can be. If the aspect is near sixty degrees, this change may be more subtle–more a change of habits you see do not match your real goals.

Jupiter/Mercury Last Quarter

Mercury is ninety to forty-five degrees behind Jupiter after the opposition.

You're the individual who has to make changes in your ways of communicating if you hope to get better results out of your position in society and out of your contacts with others. You will have to realize that sometimes you purposely stretch things; that you can be, by decision, irritating in what you have to say and sometimes go overboard in your theories.

Some of this is testing–finding out what people really do think and what truly motivates them. But some of it is just an urge to irritate, also, and you'll have to decide what you're going to do about that. You like to challenge people and if you get results from it, who can criticize you? Sometimes it's a matter of your morality and your ideas being in conflict and it's through this argumentativeness that you make decisions about changing one or the other. Your early religion and your early schooling might have been in conflict, also, and your way of getting yourself across is the result.

If the aspect is near seventy-two degrees, you're a creative communicator and the challenges you pose people are there because you cannot stand living in a rut or seeing them in one, either.

If it's near sixty degrees, you can consciously go about changing either your ideas or your morality so that they fit one another better, so that they work together rather than against one another. Common sense becomes you, and you're likely to follow it in making whatever changes are necessary in your life.

Mars/Venus Last Quarter
Venus is ninety to forty-five degrees behind Mars after opposition.

Your love life can be full of friction because you like excitement and choose to make it that way. Your desires and your basic values are in conflict because your life is going to be marked by some major changes in this department of it. You are aware, or you should be, that what you go after is not what you want and yet it might not bother you because you realize that trying something new requires a sense of adventure. It also requires changes of orientation from time to time. So what you love, and how you love, is often in a process of flux because you've chosen to make it that way. If you're the creative type, you can become very involved in the conflict of creation and the excitement that is generated by the fusion of opposites. Whatever type you are, love or creative activity is going to bring about significant changes in your life.

If the aspect is near seventy-two degrees, it's because you are learning to express your real self by going after what may not be like you until you do change. If it's near sixty degrees, you can consciously change either your values or your desire to line them up with one another so your creations and your love are productive for you–in realization and in effectiveness.

Saturn/Jupiter Last Quarter
Jupiter is ninety to forty-five degrees behind Saturn after opposition.

You are the type who must realize, at some significant point in your life, that what you've been doing for a living has got to change because it's becoming obsolete. You're the type, too, who will find your life jolted by discovering that your ideas about practicality, and your chosen ability to support yourself, are going out of style–that you require at least a change of outlook if you're going to survive in the world as it's shaping up.

You could be extremely competent in your career or profession and yet find that what you need is a challenge that takes you beyond mere competence. You're the type who could originate new ways of making a living and though you might not immediately profit from them, they could turn out to be the vanguard of what is to come. Ideas for changing the standard ways of doing things are your special possession. All you have to do is make the decision to put some actual life into them. Some of these ideas may be considered rebellious or destructive to what has worked, but that shouldn't bother you.

What should bother you is your tendency to ignore common sense at critical points of your life. The only thing that should bother you about it is that you have a choice about whether you are going to use it or ignore it. Circumstances didn't really get you into a spot; you chose to put yourself there.

If the aspect is near seventy-two degrees, you're the kind of person who finds change in the realities of life a kind of self-expression. You will undoubtedly be able to initiate highly creative new methods in the things you try to change.

If it's near sixty degrees, you can become an expert at making changes that allow a gain in productivity. You have a special sense, from observation and conscious decision, for making things work more practically. All you have to do to change what's outmoded is make the decision to work gradually into a new way, a new technique, or a new system.

Uranus/Saturn Last Quarter

Saturn is ninety to forty-five degrees behind Uranus after opposition.

It is you and people born near your birth year who will decide, long before anything really happens about it, that there is a better way to be an individual and better reasons and goals for society than those that people commonly accept. It is your task, in fact, to nurture new ideas until they can take shape in your mind, your expression, or simply life. This does not mean that they have to take expression, but they must take shape, at least mentally. You know it because of what you see around you that is dying in its obsolescence, but you often try to ignore it. And what is "it?"

It is the realization that people are caught in a rut, that they don't know any more why they do what they do, that life has become automatic and overly security-oriented. Because you observe, you can see that it is time for something new to develop. You can also sense that this lurks just beneath the surface even in those who are most pious in terms of the past and its morality. You have a choice to make: You can live, bored, in the past and its forms, or you can consciously commit yourself to supporting new ideas for the future. A divine discontent stirs in you. You should let it out, through talk or through writing. It is there, realized in you, so many who follow will change themselves and act it out. But it has to originate in consciousness somewhere and that is happening in and through you.

Prophet

Balsamic Moon:

Moon is forty-five to zero degrees behind the Sun before conjunction.

You are born in the dark of the Moon and emerge as the darkling of family or society. You hardly ever grow up to be what those who gave birth to your body or your personality ever expected. This is because you realize, at an extremely crucial and tumultuous juncture in your life, that what the past has made of you ill equips you for what demands to come to life all around you. In order to live in the future, you are going to have to make a conscious and committed decision to break with your past; to go on without it, to move forward to what is but a glimmering when you first begin to see it.

You also have to decide that though it seems you are inadequately equipped for the task, because of what you were taught when you were growing up and because of the heritage that was handed down to you, you must live the future in the present. In doing this, you can make yourself a martyr or a prophet and, most likely, both in some ways.

You are the type who knows when the time has ended for a method, a way of life, or a motivating force in people. And you must speak for what is trying to emerge from them because if someone does not, it will never have a chance for true life. You will always see and be able to say, quite clearly, what is ahead for people or for society. This will not make you popular when you first articulate it and, after a few experiences with being ostracized by your peers, you may decide to keep it quiet. If you do, life will surely become a kind of living death for you. Yes, you can function quite well in the past and you can die there quite well, too.

But what of the future? Who is going to work for its life? Who is going to take the initial actions that will lead to what everyone agrees later was necessary, after it became a fact? The answer is you. That's why the martyr is often you. Your powers of observation are acute. They stretch into the past, they objectively analyze the present, and they envision the future. This acuteness is accompanied by a vividness of purpose that galvanizes you to action when you find the vision clear and compelling. You not only can lead, but you can explain why you are leading and what the direction and goal is ahead. Often, people will only appreciate you after you have abandoned them and gone on. This is because few want to dare into what is unknown and yet once someone clears the way, they will follow. You aren't interested in them then, because you are going on.

You will find that you know many people fully and yet you know few people for very long. Each one serves a purpose in what you are doing or learning and something happens through your relationship with them. We could say these meetings and relationships are fateful. They serve a purpose and then they are over. You must always realize that though you do not have the body or the form yet, you are the future and it won't be born in body or form that matches its goal until you act for the goal, no matter how ill-equipped you are.

36 °

Moon is within orb of the thirty-six degree aspect of the Sun but still behind it. You possess special know-how and specific techniques that make your goals and your actions work together uniquely. Once you see your goal you know how to change your own quirks, inherited from the past and all it gave you that was obsolete to your purpose so that what you do fits what you're aiming toward. We could say you're technically proficient in unique ways when you want to carry something out. You are the prophet whose mannerisms fit his visions in ways that people might not understand but find compelling.

30°

Moon is within orb of the thirty degree aspect of the Sun but still behind it. You have been taught habits and emotional reactions in your early life that are going to impede your progress unless you analyze them and eliminate those of them that are not only antiquated but are blocking your full expression. This means you have to take what you've inherited and consciously recondition much of it. Until you do, you will find all kinds of impediments in your way–they aren't from outside you, they come from you.

It could also be said by a keen observer that you probably don't look like what you're saying or that you don't act like what you're urging. This is part of your makeup, however, and you will have to live with what can't be changed, but try not to let it get in your way. If nothing else, you can explain it if you analyze it carefully. This must be said because it won't be as easy for you to notice as it will for someone from the outside to see almost instantly. You should at least be aware of it and, hopefully, do something effective about it.

Saturn/Moon Balsamic
Moon is forty-five to zero degrees behind Saturn before conjunction.

Your idea of who you are and what you are doing will be highly prejudiced by the past unless you make a conscious effort to change the automatic ways in which you are impressing yourself upon others. You actually need an identity change in order to carry out what you truly believe in. This is because the ideas your parents, and even your society, drilled into you are self-destructive to the individuality which must emerge from you. Think back on it. Aren't the follies of your parents and those who taught you to be competent in society motivated by ideas which you can't really accept when you see them clearly? And what are you going to do about it? You are going to have to forge a concept of yourself and a pattern of reactions to others which match it that will allow you to operate as you'd like to operate rather than as you've been taught to operate in order to survive in a dying world or a dying idea system. Imagine what you want to project about yourself and then begin doing it.

Jupiter/Mercury Balsamic
Mercury is forty-five to zero degrees behind Jupiter after the opposition.

If you are a writer, teacher, or communicator of any form, you could be called visionary. In fact, your ways of putting yourself across to others are often shocking to them, and clearly ahead of their time—as far as other people having yet accepted them as being natural. Your ideas and your morality will probably go through at least one, and maybe several, significant changes in your lifetime. And it will be because you have decided to clear yourself of them. You are the type of person who can analyze an idea and then discover its flaws at the same time that you are envisioning one to take its place.

What is wrong with the majority's ideas and even its pieties is extremely clear to you. But what you have to do, eventually, is offer an alternative. This may not make you popular since people bleed themselves with their ideas and morals much as they did with leeches in Medieval Europe. But you will be vindicated. Later. If there is anyone who can invent or put together a new way, a new method, or a new means for communicating, it is you.

Mars/Venus Balsamic
Venus is forty-five to zero degrees behind Mars before conjunction.

If nothing else is going to be different about you, what you love and how you love obviously will be. You are the kind of person who can martyr yourself to another because you can see in him what others refuse to see. You can also martyr yourself in your peers' eyes because you believe there are new motives for loving and new ways of expressing it and somebody has to make the first move in the game that leads to general change.

Your love life may be marked by associations that occurred more for abstract reasons than for personal satisfaction. You could "go through" people because each relationship had something in it that made you grow, though none was what you needed to become attached to. If you are a creator (or even if you are a parent), you're the individual who can see the shape of the future in what you produce. What you give birth to is what the figure will be. And you will tend to love that which people do not yet appreciate but which they, like sheep, will eventually follow or accept as the norm. But it won't exist unless someone nurtures it and you are the candidate by your own choice. Your love life could be called individualistic, it could be called different and even strange; but it could never be called worthless. For you have the ability to love into being what people do not recognize they need, but which must thrive if they are not to sleep forever in their dead dreams.

Saturn/Jupiter Balsamic
Jupiter is forty-five to zero degrees behind Saturn before conjunction.

You are the type who can fail and fail again in the world's realm of practicalities–until you discover the kind of method, the way of making money, the ability to survive in reality that nobody else wants to test. You could be called crazy, but you could also originate the systems that the future demands when the past has failed.

Long after you tested it and made it feasible (but everyone rejected it because it was too far out) someone will find your system and bring it to life. And he probably won't even give you credit for it.

This indicates to me that you should never entirely abandon your experiments. The ones you made operative five years ago will probably only be appreciated now. But by now, you could have become bored with them. Still, you must realize that what intrigued you about them is that they were of the future.

The future, you must also realize, is now in two different dimensions. One is at the moment and one is in the future moment that you will experience as the now that followed its predecessor. Don't let time defeat you. It will if you follow others' concepts of it. You were meant to experience its truth–that it is ever-present but people's perceptions and acceptance of it are not. People's perceptions and acceptance are what actually change. The validity of your survival instincts requires only time to materialize; but your ideas must never stop. Some of them are timeless.

Uranus/Saturn Balsamic

Saturn is forty-five to zero degrees behind Uranus before conjunction.

What you dream, what you hope, what you envision as being the province of the individual, is what is going to come about. You may not be there when it happens in the mass, but you will be responsible for it if you do not die in the strictures of your own time and social surround¬ings.

This latter can only happen if you allow yourself, out of frustration, to live a meaningless life in order to curry popular acceptance. You, of all people, know that what's popular is about finished. There is such a thing as hollow honors and you could receive them if you killed out the spirit that informs your mind, your passions, and your urge to be more than those around you are willing to experience or simply to let live. You will have to let it live in yourself and this will shock and excite many, but it will also pave the way for people who are to come.

You may find yourself very lonely in what you are doing, but you should not listen to the past and forget that you have seen the future–

and it will surround you and vindicate you in numbers, though it's only one in you at the moment.

Your way of finding yourself will be looked at as dangerous. It will certainly disturb the status quo. But that is its only way of protecting itself–by making you feel odd and out of step. You are out of step with what's marching to the abyss, but you are in step with what's slowly emerging as the future.

You have one great talent: You can clearly formulate and lucidly articulate what is going to become the next reality. You can see it, know why it's coming, and explain its motives. That is more than what those who come to live it will be able to do. And that is what they are counting on you to do in consciousness before they emerge to give it life spontaneously.

7
Ahead and Behind

The nature of human consciousness is such that it requires reference points in order to be satisfied with its perceptions. Despite the fact that we live in a world where it is taught that human evolution is haphazard and that a human being must accomplish everything he is going to achieve in one life span of seventy to ninety years, the consciousness of most men is at least intrigued with ideas that go beyond that.

The structure of cyclic perception is such that it does give us reference points. There is a beginning to the cycle, a climax to it and a conclusion. The beginning is an emergence from something greater than experience and the conclusion is a movement to something beyond the experienced reality. A cycle doesn't emerge out of nothing and then return to nothing. It emerges from something that needed it as a reference for experience and the conclusion of the cycle leads to another such emergence.

In our time, the idea of reincarnation is beginning to make an impression on the minds of Western men, though it has existed without our belief or support for thousands of years in the minds of men who make up an actual majority of the human beings inhabiting the Earth. I will not, in this book, ask anyone to accept the traditional ideas of reincarnation. I would rather present an idea of the motivation that stands behind the cycle of experience I have so far presented in terms of planets and personality.

Yes, there is a personality that can be perceived in terms of the bodies that surround us because they are sky representatives of the bodies of psychological force that operate within us. There is a system outside, in other words, that parallels the one we find operating inside us.

The question we examine next is: What is the reason for the structure of that system? What motivates the phases of the cycle to operate as they do?

We must look at some esoteric interpretations of the planetary forces to see it clearly. If one probes into astrology enough, he is bound to come across sources who call the Sun the spirit of the human life and the Moon the body of the past (this latter often being referred to as a psychological body of habits). Thus, the lunation cycle, when taken esoterically, represents a spirit and a body coming together and its phases or steps show their interaction in a cycle of experience or growth through an intermingling of forces.

If one takes what I say literally, it must be realized that it can be applied only to the Sun/Moon cycle because the other planetary forces do not represent spirit and body though they can be taken to represent other esoteric forces in the human being. Still, awareness (spirit-Sun) and the psychological body it works through (Moon-emotion body) are represented only by Sun and Moon.

Let us consider that the phases of the lunation cycle represent a progressive series of experiences between an incarnating principle (seen in the birth chart as the Sun) and the human intelligence (seen in the birth chart as the Moon) through which it must manifest, operate, and receive cooperation. Remember that any phase of the Sun and Moon at birth is in effect in one human life for the duration of a lifetime. This view of the cycle and its motivation may give us some reasons for the quirks and characteristics of each personality type.

New Moon

This is the initial coming together of Sun and Moon. It therefore structures a whole cycle of activity which includes eight phases of building, structuring, gaining awareness, or participating in life. But this is the beginning. Step number one. If this is the beginning of a cycle of experience, it is obvious that the goal of the cycle is important. The Sun (and the degree of the zodiac at which it meets the Moon) is the key to this personality and its motivation.

In terms of reincarnation, this personality is a new projection for the incarnating principle that stands behind the activity. We could say this represents the first incarnation in a particular kind of activity; racial, social, intellectual, emotional, or spiritual experience. It could be the opening phase of a series of lives geared to some overriding goal that the incarnating principle wishes to live out.

The birth chart house in which the Sun is located represents a special kind of activity that will initiate the incarnating principle into this series of lives. The degree of the Sun indicates a goal which is extremely important. Because the Sun is what it is, the motivation of the personality is a key to his life. The house which has the sign Leo on it in the birth chart is where in the life this goal must finally be established in order that the next step in the cycle can be embarked upon. Leo means the individual expressing himself in human terms. The Leo urge to be, to express, to stamp his identity upon the awareness of others, to be known on the Earth records as an individual in his own right, is a key factor in this personality. There must be a strong projection for this is the initial projection in a series of projections that will follow upon it and move on from whatever it establishes.

Crescent Moon

This is the second phase of the great cycle and the Moon is the key to it. Once the goal has been established it must be impressed upon the psychological or emotional body in which it is going to be carried out. This requires a repolarization of habit patterns which may have been conditioned by a past series of experiences which are not appropriate to those newly focused under the preceding New Moon. The degree of the zodiac at which the New Moon occurred before birth, in this personality, shows what that goal was. The Moon's degree at birth indicates the pattern of habit which must repolarized if this phase of the cycle is to be accomplished.

The Crescent Moon personality feels ghosts around him because there are stronger memories of preceding cycles of activity than there are of this new one. But one must break from the past cycle of experience to move on. The New Moon could be called initial incarnation in a cycle of activity. But the Crescent Moon can be considered possession of the psychological, or human, body that is to experience the activity.

The house the Moon resides in at birth indicates activity in the life that will have to go through a number of changes to make the cycle effective in the life. It also shows activity in which flexibility is necessary if the past is not to overwhelm the individual. The house bearing the sign Cancer is where, in activity, the personality will eventually most strongly manifest itself to prove that it has broken from the past, that it has given birth to the new cycle of life. Esoterically, Cancer represents the womb in which life begins, in which it is given its chance to live. It is protected and nourished there until ready to emerge. The Cancer house in this birth chart provides much the same function across a cycle of projected lives or experiences.

First Quarter Moon

Once the human body (and let's view it as a psychological body rather than a physical one) has been inhabited and possessed, it must be activated to the task of the series of incarnations or experiences. This occurs in the third step. Whatever remains of the past must be liquidated from the life. The individual has the urge to become socially active to effect a new image of himself. He plunges into crisis and he is motivated by the urge to make his presence known.

The most powerful socializing factor in the astrological makeup is the planet Jupiter. Its location by house in the birth chart indicates where the individual will make his most effective impression upon society in individual activities. The house which has the sign Sagittarius on it indicates where, in activity, this social impression will eventually leave its strongest ramifications. Sagittarius in the zodiac represents the outward movement of man from his self-contained and sealed-off little community of personal fears and personal involvements.

This incarnation or experience represents the psychological man-body moving out, on the spirit of its inner motives (the New Moon degree before birth) to establish itself in the records of society or on those other records Cayce called Akasha. The zodiacal degree of Jupiter at birth can indicate the reasons for a need to establish oneself in society's records. It also indicates the motivation behind a number of crises that will mark the individual life.

Gibbous Moon

The initial step is to incarnate, the second is to take charge, the third is to move out into activity, and the fourth is to perfect the human vehicle through which the activity is being manifested. This is the goal of the Gibbous Moon life, to make it of worth within a larger framework than its own awareness of individuality. Such a task calls for a spiritual apprenticeship in life.

The planet Saturn is the shaper and teacher of the solar system. Its location by house in the birth chart indicates the kind of activities that will most have to be defined in order that the spiritual apprenticeship becomes effective in the personality. Its degree at birth is an indication of the motivation behind the personality's urge to perfection of itself as an individual. This is the final phase of the Moon under which instinct is the primary force of operation. Awareness will soon have to take charge under the Full Moon.

But now it is prepared for by training the psychological body to be of use to something greater than itself. It is necessary to perfect systems of operation in this life, but it is also necessary to see that they do not become so crystallized that they will be inflexible. This will require a depth of understanding that will be attained or avoided in the activities of this personality indicated by the house on whose cusp the sign Capricorn is found.

Capricorn represents the understanding in a human being that there are things to be rendered to Caesar (the world) and things to be rendered to God (what we could call the greater whole and, in this case, the incarnating principle which is now rising up to the point where it will eventually take conscious charge of the operations in the series of incarnations left to experience). The degree on the cusp of the tenth house will show how the individual can receive and incorporate spiritual energy into his life. The degree on the cusp of the fourth house will show how he can make his way through life in worldly security as he does this.

Full Moon

This is the turning point in the whole cycle of experience (or incarnation, if you prefer). The fifth step is the one in which man, having experienced himself and proven it capable of something greater, begins to allow mind, not brain, to guide him.

It is at this point in the cycle of incarnation that illumination must be gained or a compact made between incarnating principle and psychological body. They must become aware of one another and must work together or there is no reason to continue. It is really the soul urge or the incarnating principle of life that the Full Moon person seeks to know.

The typical personality of that phase searches desperately for his soul mate, as he might call it, or for the perfect match in a relationship. And it is inside, awaiting his recognition. The planet Mercury as representative of spiritual mind (representative because it is the carrier of the messages, not the originator) rather than the physical brain indicates the purpose of awareness in this life. The house it occupies indicates the experiences in life that will most bring about this awareness. The house that has Gemini on its cusp shows where in life activities the awareness can most effectively be applied in small matters and the house that has Virgo on its cusp shows where in activity the awareness can be organized into a systematic approach to the world beyond small matters. The degree of the Full Moon before birth is an indication of how awareness will be most fully realized in this personality's activities in life.

Disseminating Moon

This is the sixth of the experiences in a cycle of the incarnating principle's activities and this is the apex of the whole cycle. After incarnation, possession, activation, perfection, and awareness of what is to be done, it is now time to do it.

After his mind has become a channel to awareness, the personality's heart becomes a channel to motivation and the planet Venus, which represents both individual and social values in the personality, becomes emphasized. It is the key to whether the individual will or will not carry out what the principle is trying to manifest in life through him. Its degree at birth shows the motivation behind the values the individual will adopt in this life to go about making his living worthwhile. The house Venus occupies indicates activity that can transform personal values to the task.

The house that has Taurus on its cusp indicates where in life personal love can be utilized best. The house that has Libra on its cusp shows where social values will be manifested most strongly if the incarnation is to be effective. The degree of the Full Moon before birth indicates the reason for the search in which every Disseminating Moon personality is engaged to find an effective message to live out in the presence of others. This life is crucial. It is what all the others were geared toward. What the individual feels, what he loves, and what motivates him in his actions are also crucial. If Venus truly is the beautiful part of the human that most astrologers make it, this is the personality that can most effectively demonstrate it. His values and what he does with them are everything.

Last Quarter Moon

This is the seventh step and the one where the personality realizes it must begin looking inward rather than outward. Whatever was to be accomplished in the cycle of experiences or incarnations has been accomplished or defeated. It is now time to repolarize the existence so that the incarnating principle may free itself of attachment to a particular body or task.

For the personality, this will require that he begin listening to something other than the ego which is represented in astrology by the planets from Saturn inward to the Sun. Now, the intelligence must let in flashes of perception from the representative of the greater wholeness that accompanies the personality in life. The greater wholeness is what we call, psychologically, the unconscious. When one steps into it he is in the realm of Neptune (spiritual creativity, just as Jupiter is social creativity) and Pluto (spiritual role, just as Saturn is human role or task).

But to get there he must cross the bridge that Uranus represents. The degree of Uranus at birth indicates how this crossing from ego-con-sciousness into the realm of the incarnating principle's awareness, will be effected.

The house Uranus occupies at birth will show the activities that can most effectively allow the crossing. The house that has Aquarius on the cusp will indicate where the changed consciousness, after this crossing can be most effective in life activity. Uranus is always speaking to us, but our Saturn-bound minds often do not choose to listen. The Last Quarter Moon personality must listen inside himself, and go about a process of recreation inside himself. He must want to be worthwhile to something greater than his own self-satisfaction. Listening to Uranus is the key to finding out how to go about it.

The degree of the progressed New Moon after birth will show what this can lead to in the early life. The degree of the progressed New Moon after age thirty will indicate what it can lead to in middle life. What is required is a reorientation of the existence to some goal that is beyond that which was taught the person early in life by parents and society. This life is almost like listening to intimations of the future. And making oneself ready so he can participate in it.

Balsamic Moon

This is the dark of the Moon before the next New Moon and it is the last of the experiences or incarnations in the series by the incarnating principle. It is a kind of winding up of what's left over from the previous experiences, but it is much more. It is the conscious commitment of the psychological body to destroy itself, in form, so that it can be reconsti¬tuted to a new spiritual task.

The one thing in the human personality that is most powerful or most destructive to the individual is the desire nature. It is represented astrologically by the planet Mars. If there is one thing that has to be changed or geared up to a new task, it is the desires of the personality. So the planet Mars becomes powerful in the makeup of the Balsamic Moon person.

Its zodiacal degree indicates the nature of the experiences that can re-polarize the physical and emotional energies so they will not only agree to, but participate in the task of envisioning the next step and the new psychological body in this current life, which is an end of an old cycle of activity. While the personality goes about straightening up loose ends it must also gear itself to the task that is ahead.

The house in which Mars is located at birth indicates activities that must be repolarized to what is ahead. The house which bears on its cusp the sign Scorpio shows activities that will be transformed in their nature if this repolarization is effective in the life. The Balsamic Moon person is often an effective prophet because he has a passion for what is ahead, because he desires to see it come about. If he is not going to be simply a dead end to something that is finished, that is effectively over, then his life must take decisive directions toward the future at each New Moon after his birth. The Balsamic Moons after birth will be important too because it is in these that he will see the shape of the future in life that must be lived out if he is to approach at the end of this life the road that lies beyond.

There are lots of nasty things said in astrology about the planet Mars and the sign Scorpio, but this is an indication of the spiritual mindset of the state to which man has currently evolved. Mars may be ruthless and even self-destructive, operating in a meaningless, goalless life. But when it is applied to a task, there is no greater power to be harnessed. So the Mars of the Balsamic Moon personality and its engine of desire to reach a new start of existence is a powerful key to the initiation of a new cycle of activity which will occur under the next New Moon or the next manifestation on Earth of the incarnating principle. But it is the energy of Mars and the psychological power of the sign Scorpio that is required to set the new cycle in motion out of the old one.

(In the interpretation I have constantly alluded to zodiacal degrees. I am referring to a specific set of them. They are the Sabian symbols. None of the other symbol interpretations make sense when applied as I have suggested here. But the Sabian set, particularly the one outlined as it is in Dane Rudhyar's *An Astrological Mandala* is specially geared to his kind of view.

The Moving Energy Flow Index

A and B are any two objects (planets) moving on the celestial circle. They meet at the beginning of the cycle and then B, the faster of the two, moves on to create the cycle of energy flow that is diagrammed on the circle. Each phase of the cycle begins at the large numbered degree and its total meaning contains the meaning of the aspects (smaller numbers) that fall within it and the space of the next large number. This cycle goes on between any two planets in the sky, with the periods between their conjunctions being longer or shorter. A is the reference point even though it is moving. B is the faster of the two, making the cycle possible

www.ingramcontent.com/pod-product-compliance
Lightning Source LLC
Chambersburg PA
CBHW051947160426
43198CB00013B/2336